WELLNESS INCORPORATED

JENNIFER BUCHANAN

WELLNESS INCORPORATED

The Health Entrepreneur's Handbook

ISBN 978-0-9739446-3-1 (paperback)
ISBN 978-0-9739446-4-8 (ebook)

Produced by Page Two
www.pagetwostrategies.com
Cover design by Teresa Bubela
Interior design by Nayeli Jimenez

19 20 21 22 23   5 4 3 2 1

www.wellnessincorporated.ca

*To my younger self, and to all the other entrepreneurs
who dream of making a difference.*

"Do not go where the path may lead;
go instead where there is no path and leave a trail."

RALPH WALDO EMERSON

CONTENTS

THE HEART OF THE WORK

NOT TOO LONG ago, I invited five professionals to my office to put my business to the test. I had met each of them in different situations, and I greatly respected their insights, perspectives, and business acumen.

At the time, I had owned my business for more than twenty years. I had loyal staff and plenty of clients, but I was uncertain my music therapy company was viable, let alone sustainable for another twenty years. We had low profit margins, and I continued to work many long hours just as I had done when I started the company. I carefully looked to these individuals for help in making a difficult decision: close our doors or move into the next phase of growth.

I presented every aspect of my company's journey, using case studies and statistics to define our growth and show our financial status and forecast. During the last ten minutes of the presentation I showed a video that I often share with potential customers, about the people we serve and how our offerings have affected their lives. When I turned the lights back on, my guests were crying. Many times before, I had witnessed tears after describing the effects of our work, but I was caught off guard when these seasoned business leaders heard the facts and felt the emotions that went along with our work.

Because I was reflecting on the emotional impact of the video, I almost missed what the group was telling me: "Yes," they said. At first, I was confused and then remembered that I had asked them a question at the beginning of the presentation—before I shared the mission statement and SWOT (strengths, weaknesses, opportunities, threats) analysis, before the profit-and-loss statements and client testimonials. I had asked them if the way I was operating this business seemed sustainable to them, something that could continue in a similar way for many more years to come. "Yes," they said and then they followed up with questions, to which I responded:

Are you in debt? No.

Do you pay your staff? Yes, we have contractors and staff on annual salary with modest benefits.

Do you pay yourself? Yes, I have been on salary for the past decade.

Are your customers happy with your services? Yes.

And finally: *Are you still getting regular referrals?* Yes, and we are seeing growth every year; in fact, we have been adding almost one new employee every year since the day we opened our doors.

For the first time in a long time, I heard my answers as validation of our company's achievements and not as evidence of its weaknesses.

When family members or friends asked me similar questions earlier in my business development, my answers were quite different. Then, I knew the services we provided were making a difference in people's lives, but I didn't always pay myself the way I should and I didn't feel I was always providing the best service to my customers, giving them the time and energy they deserved. My discomfort with these shortcomings troubled me a lot and helped me begin to change many of our actions and processes, which carried us into our current reality.

When we faced a new problem or a recurring one, I wanted to figure it out. I had a sense of what the right answers were and where we needed to be, but I still lacked all the skills I needed to get there. I rarely spoke about the "business" side of my company with others because I was worried it would somehow discredit the overarching good work we were doing. I didn't want to share my failings with anyone for fear that my dream would stop before it really got going.

But on this day, I heard the answers differently and felt something shift inside myself.

This group heard the heart of the work and understood that my company was making a difference in the community it served. They also felt that, because of its consistent (albeit modest) positive cash flow, my company had become financially sustainable, even successful. They felt that with a few more tweaks, coupled with a significant shift in mindset on my part, I could carry on in a new way and make an even grander difference.

At this meeting, I learned that my lack of confidence wasn't originating from what *was* happening but from the fear of what *might* happen: the fear that I could no longer serve the clients I wanted to serve, the fear that I would have to close my company's doors, the fear that I would have to give up on my dream—and I equated that fear with reality.

To take the next step, I had to cast aside my notions of how my business "ought to be," by other people's standards. Instead, I needed to build my business as it was meant to be: one that would thrive through the rough patches, serve the community, and help clients reach their goals. I had to embrace a new perspective, a more optimistic learning state that would continue to open doors and allow me to feel a true sense of purpose. It was important that I continue to forge a new path for my values-driven business and myself, committing to the long haul. In many ways, this moment was a reckoning and a way of bringing me full circle—to my beginnings as a young music therapist in Calgary, Canada, searching for my first client.

Finding My Place

EARLY IN MY career, there were no music therapy jobs in the public healthcare sector. To access the clients I wanted to serve, I had to create a model to reach them, so I started a private, mobile, community-based business. The company would commute to where its customers were, learn their interests and goals, and treat them in their current environment (hospital, care home, agency). Over several years, as I hired staff, I began to embrace my expanding role of leading a team, developing systems, and learning the ins and outs of running a growing business.

Over time, I noticed a disparity of practice and language between the healthcare and education environments I served and what I was hearing at the business networking groups I had joined. I was learning from my clients, and the healthcare and education environments I was working in, that a different style of "doing business" was needed.

I have always identified with the word *entrepreneur*, but at times it seemed to describe someone who was more adventurous and risk-taking than I ever felt. Much later in my career, I heard the term *social entrepreneur*, referring to an individual who cares about, and finds solutions for, pressing social problems, needs, and challenges. I felt aligned with much of social entrepreneurship, and terms from this growing movement struck a chord with me: *social impact, community impact,* and *social purpose business*. However, working in a relatively new healthcare profession, one that I was passionate about and wanted to help spread throughout North America and the world, I felt the terminology of social entrepreneurship was still not quite on point for me.

> "Whenever society is stuck or has an opportunity to seize a new opportunity, it needs an entrepreneur to see the opportunity and then to turn that vision into a realistic idea and then a reality and then, indeed, the new pattern all across society. We need such entrepreneurial leadership at least as much in education and human rights as we do in communications and hotels."
>
> **BILL DRAYTON,**
> **founder of Ashoka: Innovators for the Public**

Healthcare and wellness companies needed a new term that described our unique business model, which focused on health and wellness, serving clients in both public and private sectors.

I couldn't find any resources to show me how an entrepreneur in the health and wellness field could build a sustainable business without compromising their organization's patient-focused goals and mission. Many books helped me with starting up, closing sales, and advertising my services, but I always found that the language didn't fit a health service business like mine. There were plenty of books on building businesses, sure; lots of resources for aspiring and current entrepreneurs; and even a growing field of information for the social entrepreneur. But nothing for a socially minded entrepreneur working in healthcare.

It took me over two decades to define how I saw myself within the business community, the healthcare community, the non-profit community, and the vast populations we served. I started to feel we *are* different. We are offering a new way of doing business: *a health entrepreneur's way.*

Who Is a Health Entrepreneur?

A HEALTH ENTREPRENEUR is the owner, and many times the operator, of a private health-service business. The health entrepreneur's services are within the spectrum of health, wellness, and wellness education. The health entrepreneur serves the public's needs and interests, helping clients reach their desired health and wellness goals through their core service as healthcare professionals, including therapists, wellness coaches, counsellors, naturopaths, community home-care providers, as well as other specialists in areas of preventative health and recovery.

Health entrepreneurs, through their services and business practices, are uniquely positioned to break through many barriers and bring necessary social change and care to individual citizens and communities. When making decisions, health entrepreneurs take a "people first" approach based not on financial transactions but on relationships and desired outcomes.

Looking back, I see it as a privilege to be part of a much larger change within many systems—health care, education, and business. Across the board, we are turning toward different ways of living, caring, and doing good work. I see the success of the health entrepreneur's business as essential for a healthy society. It is, therefore, critical that more resources and supports be put in place to help these businesses connect with their clients and patients in a way that inspires the client, helping health entrepreneurs to be the best they can be for many years to come.

Who Is This Book For?

THIS BOOK IS for you, the entrepreneur who strives to do better in society and in your own business. You might not identify with the term health entrepreneur (yet), but by reading this book you'll realize that the meaning of the term fits. You are a private practitioner, for-profit-for-purpose business owner, healthcare advocate, or health-service business owner who aspires to make a living *and* make a difference. You're a business leader who considers both the social and financial bottom lines, but always prioritizes customer care and service. For all our focus on social objectives, health entrepreneurs are still entrepreneurs at heart, solving problems and initiating useful ideas to ensure quality and positive outcomes within one of every nation's biggest necessities: healthcare.

THIS BOOK INTRODUCES nine principles that I believe every entrepreneur should consider as they develop their business:

1. **Drive your dream.** At the heart of every business is the dream, the mission to be shared with the world. A business that focuses on community impact measures its success not by revenue but by the difference it makes. Sharing this difference is truly the heart of the work for the health entrepreneur. Applying a mindset that breaks through barriers of worry and low confidence is critical for the health entrepreneur's success.

2. **Strengthen your expertise.** Focusing on weaknesses only brings increased anxiety and feelings of inadequacy. Being an expert in your field offers many benefits. You feel more confident and believe in your ability to succeed, which increases your likelihood of success, as well as your reputation, network, and credibility. To become an expert requires investment and a commitment to lifelong learning.

3. **Maximize your message.** I have been reminded frequently that "if your company is not growing, it's dying." For the health entrepreneur, developing a meaningful message and plan that will gain momentum over time can be far more important than focusing on profits. When the health entrepreneur executes their messaging strategy well, they share their dream, and the company's expertise attracts more customers.

4. **Scale for impact.** Scaling can be the most difficult part of growing any company. Entrepreneurs, in general, tend to think big, and at some point, scaling becomes vital to

maximize the desired impact. Managing finances, including cash flow and profit usage, are critical during this stage. The health entrepreneur draws strength from their mission, leading to growth.

5. **Build in the spirit of equity.** Equality—as well-intentioned as its pursuit may be—often mistakenly assumes that we begin at the same starting line and is often misunderstood as "treating everyone the same." Equity is when everyone has the resources and tools they need to feel equal. When you infuse a spirit of equity into your business opportunities, everyone experiences freedom from barriers.

6. **Clear the path.** Without the right mindset, everything becomes more difficult than it needs to be—and may at times seem impossible. Mindset determines the choices we believe we have, and these choices determine what we decide. The right mindset, which can be understood as a clear path, helps health entrepreneurs move from feeling stuck to seeing a way forward.

7. **Secure your health.** Promoting wellness in yourself, in the company culture, and among the entire team brings vibrancy and longevity to the services you provide. When running a health-centred business, it's vital to prioritize self-care in order to achieve greater outcomes. The better we feel, the better work we provide. The better work we do, the greater our impact.

8. **Find your *blisspoint*.** Used more commonly in the formulation of food products, the blisspoint is the ratio of ingredients, such as salt, sugar, and fat, to optimize deliciousness. The blisspoint of a health-service business is

the perfect blend of values, which fuels your good work. Identifying the values junction will bring clarity to decision making, contributing to a feeling of bliss.

9. **Leave a legacy ahead.** Leaving a legacy is about giving the best of yourself until the very end, never letting the challenges or the difficult decisions diminish your good work. The health entrepreneur is inspired by the fact that what is done today will continue to impact people in the future. It's not what we leave behind; it's what we leave ahead.

What Can I Expect to Gain?

YOU WILL GARNER several things in reading this book:

- Each chapter of *Wellness Incorporated* breaks down the above principles in detail, with concepts and ideas for you to consider through every stage of your business development.

- The Health Entrepreneur's Rx in each chapter offers pro tips that will make the principles and actions much more personal and meaningful.

- This health entrepreneur's prescription is followed by an Impact Story featuring a socially conscious company that is fulfilling its mission.

- Each chapter ends with three questions about your own business. Take time to answer them, mentally or in writing, or better yet download *Wellness Incorporated: The Health Entrepreneur's Workbook*, which outlines exercises to guide you through each chapter, challenging you along the way: www.wellnessincorporated.ca.

My hope is that each chapter, each step, provides a new perspective on your work as a health entrepreneur, and helps you remain passionate about your business, even through the inevitable difficult times. This book is not so much about how to build a business as it is a guide to help you find the magic formula for your unique company. *Wellness Incorporated* will help you with the necessary decisions along the way, ensuring that you achieve the difference you dream of making.

DRIVE YOUR DREAM

"If you don't dare to try and chase your dreams,
you'll rob yourself the joy of doing it."
SERENA WILLIAMS

LOOKING FOR A constant to guide you through the good and bad times? It's time for you to drive your dream. This chapter is about the importance of recognizing and defining your dream and sharing it with others so it influences the future, transforming lives along the way. You'll learn how to identify your personal core value, define your company's mission, and feature a memorable signature story. These foundational practices are instrumental to realizing your dream. Each element will ensure that you find the right people who are on board with your business, including but not limited to: your accountant, mentor, business coach, family members, prospective staff, and, of course, new clients.

To help us through this chapter, let's first define the four key concepts:

1. **The dream.** This is a cherished aspiration, ambition, or ideal. Your dream could be opening a therapy practice or a yoga studio, or becoming a wellness educator.

2. **The mission.** This is a formal summary of the aims and values of an organization or individual. A mission statement clearly articulates what your business is about and what it aims to do.

3. **The core value.** This is a person's primary principle, showing what is most important in their life. It is the "top feeling" behind why the health entrepreneur desires to pursue their dream. For some business owners, this can be a spiritual value; for others, it is a character trait, such as bringing more kindness into the world. For me, it is about fostering feelings of meaningful connection.

4. **The signature stories.** These are narratives that inspire and provide direction. As they are retold, signature stories gain momentum and attraction. The health entrepreneur's earliest signature story represents the spark, the trigger, to their dream.

Define Your Dream

YOU MIGHT HAVE heard of the Big Hairy Audacious Goal, or BHAG, a term coined by Jim C. Collins and Jerry I. Porras. They define a BHAG as a goal that is "clear and compelling, needing little explanation; people get it right away."[1] A BHAG feels just within reach *if* you really give it your all, working with focus and determination for the next five to ten years. Collins and Porras cite the dream to put a human on the moon as a

BHAG. Your dream needn't be quite so ambitious, but it should stretch you and challenge your belief in what you're capable of achieving.

The dream is the cornerstone of any business, regardless of its size. When you step into the role of entrepreneur, especially as the founding owner, you are essentially claiming your spot as a trailblazer or leader within your industry and community, thereby contributing to something greater than yourself. You represent the dream to yourself, your staff, and clients.

Defining the dream sounds simple, but when coupled with writing a mission statement, and setting the culture and trajectory of your company, it becomes the most critical factor of building a business. Your dream is your North Star, helping you to course-correct when you stray off track. A business's dream typically starts with one person: you, whether as CEO, owner, or founder. Your dream is the best possible future you can imagine. It feels bright, shiny, vibrant, and just about possible. It should be a stretch but not unobtainable. It feels like something worth doing and doing well.

You know that you have found your dream when the images become crystal clear—you can see or feel exactly what it will be like when you succeed. You can feel the atmosphere, see the spark in people's eyes, sense the buzz in the room, or spot the relief on your client's face; in brief, you see the impact your business is going to make.

Here is how a dream begins to formulate:

- It always starts with a niggling thought or feeling about something you find meaningful.

- Then you begin to feel it more often and it seems to increase in its cyclical revolutions through your thoughts.

- Then, one day, you may be working at your laptop, drinking a coffee, or taking a walk when your mind begins to wander unexpectedly back to the initial niggling, and a few more images appear.

- A complete idea begins to form and you feel excited.

- You know that the feeling is ready to turn into a reality when something in your external environment reflects what you've been thinking (through a comment, an image, a story, a conversation), providing insight into the next step and validating your dream.

- The last step is that you can define your dream in a concise sentence or two and feel confident when you do.

Write Your Mission

IN THOSE VERY first few weeks of starting my business in 1991, I didn't have a mission written down, though I instinctively felt the dream, and it was really big and exciting. I envisioned every one of my future clients, from two months to 104 years old, and how music therapy would affect their lives.

A mission statement is the written expression of your dream, articulated in a few lines. Constructing a mission statement takes focus, creativity, and time. A mission statement must speak to your customers, define your service, and clarify why you do what you do. It must also speak to and inspire you.

The following mission statement was the first one that really made me pay attention to my own.

The Elephant Sanctuary is a natural-habitat refuge where sick, old, and needy elephants can once again walk the Earth in peace and dignity.

The emotional impact of a mission statement must reflect the emotional content of the mission itself. At JB Music Therapy, we have always valued that our team has dedicated their education and life to this field. They are driven to help others reach their health goals. We wanted to convey our intention and essence, and distinguish ourselves in the field. We also didn't want our statement to be too long. The end result:

Through excellence in clinical practice and education, JB Music Therapy's mission is to transform lives, one note at a time.

Identify Your Core Value

VALUES FUEL YOUR mission. In chapter 6 we will visit the values of your company in order to find your blisspoint. To begin considering values, I would like you to think about your core value. A core value is the fundamental belief of the business owner. Your core value contributes greatly to the lens through which you view your business every day. Here's my core value:

My core value is believing in the power of transformational connection and that I have a role in making it happen—connection to music, connection to our agency partners, connection to our clients and their families, and the team's connection to one another.

Knowing the dream leads to defining your company's mission. Knowing your personal core value reminds you why you want to see it come to fruition. Without being in touch with a strong mission, an owner and team may not have sufficient motivation to complete a project and to persevere when things get tough. When you speak the mission out loud, it should bring a sense of belonging, reminding you of your dream, and putting you in immediate touch with your core value.

In fully living our company's mission and feeling my core value, I found myself fighting for every person's right to connect to "their good" whatever that may be, regardless of what they had been through in the past, what they were facing in the present, or what was coming at them in the future. For some, "their good" was being more comfortable, feeling less pain, more motivated, brighter, or better able to fall asleep.

Helping my clients connect to their good came easily; learning over time how to connect to "my company's good" would take a bit longer.

Live Your Mission

FOR YEARS I kept my dream inside, letting it out in bits and pieces. I did this for a few reasons: I was still getting to know the mission myself, I wasn't sure if what I dreamed could ever become a reality, and I was concerned about putting myself in an even more vulnerable position than the one I felt I was in already. However, keeping the mission secret led to many anxious nights and hours of "whirring" (a combination of worry and spiralling). On top of that, I was focused on trying to please everyone, including my young team and my new clients. These two energy-intensive activities kept me from spreading the dream as effectively as I could have in the early days.

The late Warren Bennis, a pioneer in leadership studies, said that "at the heart of every great group is a shared dream."[2] When one of my business mentors encouraged me to close my eyes and envision our ideal clients, and when I began to describe these clients out loud, imagining the benefits they would reap from interacting with us, I could feel my business begin to grow, even though I was still sitting in my chair. To get to this place of believing, then sharing, and finally living it, you first need to build the right support network for you. For me, this took time. I didn't always have the right mentor. I tested a few coaches. I got to know a few different networks. I joined a couple of boards. It took time to hire the right staff, on-board them with the necessary tools they needed (including understanding the mission and their role in it), retain the right team, and match them with the right clients. Each of these tests and steps was critical to finding the best path, and connections, to spread the dream.

Since the health entrepreneur's decisions are not driven by profit but by purpose, the mission needs to be very clearly defined and every employee needs to understand it completely. Writing about it is a start, but actually living it boldly every day is a much more powerful message. Then, when a crisis hits, the culture is so entrenched in everyone's way of working that it will be applied, even in extremely challenging situations.

Unfortunately, far too often, mission statements pay empty lip service to values that aren't lived every day by the leaders of an organization. The impact of being distanced from your mission can be felt most during an economic downturn, when the company and its team are grappling with what to hold on to. Without a compelling mission, the owner and team members may not have sufficient motivation to persevere. For organizations to be successful, the team must feel they are moving toward the same meaningful goal, a fulfilling purpose, a reason to be doing what they are doing. This sense of living the big dream through our everyday work is becoming even more relevant with our Millennial workforce.

A 2017 report by American Express surveyed 1,363 Millennials (those born between 1980 and 1996) plus 1,062 Gen Xers (born between 1965 and 1979) from the U.S., U.K., France, and Germany. More than one-third defined success as doing work that has a positive impact on society.[3]

So how do you identify the positive impact of culture, and how do you bring it to life? There is no better way for the CEO to actively and daily engage in their desired mindset than by keeping the spotlight on the dream. This means reviewing your mission and strategic plan on a regular basis, ensuring both key pieces are aligned. It means sharing your dream on a regular basis in conversation, in print, and throughout the brand of your company.

Being part of "something bigger" amounts to feeling a sense of personal responsibility and belonging for customers and co-workers. For example, when one of my staff had a sudden death in her family, the rest of the staff came together to ensure her client caseload was swiftly covered, while also connecting with the employee through emotional and physical support, thereby providing evidence of our core value.

Living the dream is not just about posting your mission statement on your company website or in the staff room; it's about embodying the core values and mission, every day, in all aspects of the company.

Commit to Your Code

A CULTURE CODE, or similar manifesto, can be a useful tool when you are beginning to integrate staff into your company. Daniel Coyle popularized this term in his book *The Culture Code*.[4] He discusses how culture is not something you are—it's something you do. I suggest that although a culture code is something that is developed, it has to start somewhere and the best place to start is based on your core value. Regardless of whether you are a solopreneur or a small business owner, settle on "a way" that you do business, based on your character and the dream you hope to achieve.

To identify your culture code, complete the following statement: "In everything we do, we believe in..."

Once you have completed this sentence, ensure it resonates with every document used in your company, including your mission statement, key success factors (by which you measure your success), and strategies (the steps to reach this success). I'll address the success factors and strategies in more detail in chapter 4, when we discuss scaling your business and growing it for optimum impact.

By working on this statement with your team and keeping the needs and values of your clients at the forefront of your mission development, you will have a tool that can help guide your next decision. When moving through a trouble spot, make sure your team knows the spirit in which you want the problem worked out. This is confirmation that the dream has saturated your entire organization—when the problem solving reflects your mission and core values.

A larger company such as the airline WestJet can help educate us on the important culture-code process.[5] WestJet intentionally imprints their mission on new staff during an initial two-day orientation process. Their culture revolves around a basic principle that happy employees mean happy customers and happy customers mean good business, which in turn makes it easier to keep employees happy.

Their statement could look something like: "In everything we do, we believe in making sure everyone is happy."

The idea is to get the WestJetters to fully engage in their desired culture, to buy into their mission, and to participate actively in making it a reality for everyone again and again.

To do that, prospective employees are exposed to the West-Jet culture before they start working for the company. When applicants research job opportunities on the company's website, they view proprietary videos that feature WestJet's values. When they start work, they participate in an orientation program that welcomes new employees and shares "the WestJet vision." The goal is to create an individual sense of ownership of the greater mission.

The consulting firm Culturology talks about this process as "meaning amplification."[6] When you amplify your dream, you amplify your message, and when you amplify your message, you amplify your impact. Individuals who feel connected to the bigger dream demonstrate stronger connections to the clients and customers they serve. In turn, the stronger the entrepreneur feels to those client connections, the more meaningful the dream.

Mark Arnoldy, former CEO of Possible Health, worked with a team that is spread out in the mountains and valleys of Nepal doing challenging work. To ensure that the company's purpose of providing "high-quality, low-cost healthcare to the world's poor" remains at the core of everything they do, he co-created a "for-impact culture code" with his team.[7] First, he asked everyone for their input. Then he put the feedback together in the form of a purpose statement and a list of guiding principles. A powerful culture code can become the basis for other documents that help guide the employees and management, such as a management manual or an employee appraisal guide. Even a recruitment process can be informed by the culture code so that the organization hires people who are a good fit culturally. That way, new hires can easily assimilate the mission of the company.

The dream you imprint is a great story, reflective of your culture code, your business manifesto. This story needs to be based on the spark that lit the big dream you hope to achieve. It should capture your values and your culture. Let's talk about how to craft a story for your business.

Determine Your Signature Story

THE BEST MARKETING tool you will ever use are signature stories that emphasize your mission, your services, the individuals you hope to serve, and your values. Your stories will not only sell your services but will also help you, the entrepreneur, remember your dream when you need it most. Taking time to craft your signature story is one of the best exercises any entrepreneur can do, especially in the early stages. You can then refer to it often when you need a dose of inspiration.

Angela Randolph, assistant professor in Entrepreneurship at Babson College in Massachusetts explains why stories may be a good means of connecting us to the dream of our business. She says, "Emotions and motivations shape cognition, which is why good stories stay with us." She goes on to say that "people are more likely to remember emotional information than non-emotional."[8] But shaping a story to really grab and hold people's attention requires time and craftsmanship to create the narrative. She suggests that every good story needs strong imagery and continuous tension. In music language, this tension is created by the way the vocalist uses tempo, volume, and rhythm to craft the story they are sharing. It is the variance in the way you convey your message that will lure the audience's attention in its lift and lull.

I start every presentation with my earliest signature story, the one of how I unknowingly entered my new profession after my grandmother asked me to learn my grandfather's favourite song and perform it at his long-term care facility. It is a speech I have made hundreds of times, and it emphasizes the huge impact of music on people's lives, including those that society sometimes forgets about, but it also reminds the entire audience about the value of connection in every aspect of their lives. Every time I tell the story, I end it with Granny's words of encouragement, "Keep going, dear." I will share this story in chapter 3, when I encourage you to craft a signature story.

The Health Entrepreneur's Rx: Launch Your Dream

EARLY IN MY career, I was so consumed by my passion and the dream of what I hoped to accomplish that the details required to get there only seemed to get in the way. I had no problem defining my dream and coming up with the mission statement; but the implementation challenged me.

It didn't take me long to realize that my aspirations meant pushing past many obstacles, working long hours, and mitigating bottlenecks and barriers—basically, the pesky details. At times these details were stumbling blocks that caused undue drama and stress. It would take time, but I eventually learned to fall in love with the details so my business could become the fully operational, useful, busy, well-recognized, and for-purpose company it was meant to be.

The ability to see the end first has come naturally to me. Seeing the final outcome, the fulfilment of the mission, inspires me. Even when I was in elementary school I remember being thrilled, almost giddy, whenever my teacher announced that our next assignment was a "major project." I could envision the final outcome quickly: the written presentation, the colours I would use on the art board, the final speech I would make to the class, and the significant point I wanted to get across. You may have known other project nerds like me.

The dream of what is possible, that thing to strive for, has always been a beacon that helps me move and take the next steps to reach my goals—even though things do not always happen exactly as I see them. Over time, and especially over this last decade, I have learned to appreciate the stumbling blocks and see them much more as building blocks, although they rarely feel that way in the moment. Here are three suggestions to keep you on mission and to help you move through the blocks that may present themselves.

Do just one thing. In an entrepreneur's day, there always seems to be one more thing to do. There are many little projects along the way and the big project never seems done. On many days, I have felt tired, even worn out, struggling to get through all the items that needed to be checked off the list. On those days, besides feeling like I needed a personal assistant, I learned to pick one thing. As someone who always has a long list of to-dos, the "one thing" rule feels more attainable. I mean, how hard can just one thing be? And often when I focus on just one thing at a time, I get a lot more done than I could have anticipated.

Embrace your inner motivator. Resources can help you to organize yourself and your day. However, you still need to motivate yourself to fully show up. The best part about starting my business at twenty-one was that my youthful optimism was at its peak. I focused purely on getting my business up and running and never considered the amount of work ahead of me. So I challenge you to embrace your inner motivator and begin to break through the belief that there is too much to do. When you own a business, there is always something to do, and for that let's be grateful—fulfilling the mission is worth it.

Move your dream ahead. Some days the next move may be a half step and other days a giant leap—but the movement will make a significant impact on the good work you are doing. Several factors will set you up for business success, but it's important to keep your business in motion, regardless of what stage you are at or how many hurdles you may need to jump.

A good friend once told me how he navigates rush hour. He said that during those busy times, he takes the longest and windiest route possible because at least then he keeps moving. In the movement, he feels he can stay calm, and although he probably drives farther, he never feels like he is being repeatedly trapped. The destination remains in sight.

So how do we keep moving every day—especially on the days our energy is depleted? When we blend our general mindset (chapter 6) with our self-care (chapter 7), movement will happen, and movement in a business like ours, on the outside looks an awful lot like work—really good work.

Impact Story: Bombas, The Sock Guys

How Sharing Your Dream
Takes You to Maximum Impact

WITH A NAME derived from the Latin word for bumblebee, Bombas believes in "a hive" that works together and makes the world a better place. Their mantra is "bee better." They weave their slogan on the inside of every pair of Bombas socks as a reminder to their customers that their mission is to help someone in need with their purchase and that small acts can add up to a big difference.[9]

After learning that socks were the number one most-requested clothing item at homeless shelters, Randy Goldberg and David Heath felt the pull to do something. For every pair that is purchased, their company donates a pair to someone in need. This model has become a popular strategy in which it is easy for consumers to understand that with their purchase, they're helping to make a great social impact: I buy one, they give one.

Donating socks is limited by hygienic issues: socks need to be new, and unfortunately, there aren't enough donations coming in to meet the demand. "I didn't grow up dreaming of being in the sock business," Goldberg stated. But once he and Heath learned about the need for good socks, they quickly formed their dream and mission.

Bombas understood that to spread this dream of helping others, their business needed to have even greater imagination. Yes, they were going to help others, but to do so they first had to design, as they said, "the best sock in the history of feet."

Heath and Goldberg realized that socks had been largely the same for decades—the sock industry hadn't been innovating, and not much had changed about the everyday sock. "We decided to start there—have a customer-focused approach to innovate and create a great sock," Goldberg said.

After investing more than a year in research and development, learning how to innovate the sock, they landed on what they felt was a great product. In August 2013, they launched an Indiegogo campaign that reached over $140,000 in pre-sales, and in 2014, the duo appeared on *Shark Tank* (similar to *Dragons' Den* in Canada), where they landed a deal. From there, things really started to grow.[10]

That growth led to the achievement of the team's initial mission: to give away as many socks as they could to those in homeless shelters around the country. When Bombas first got started, they hoped to give away one million socks by 2025. But because of the incredible reception from consumers across the globe, they hit that lofty goal much earlier. Today, they give away more than one thousand pairs a day.

By making first-rate products and providing exceptional customer service, Bombas plans to keep fulfilling their mission to give socks to those in need, using great design and a steadfast commitment to giving back—all while building around them a supportive customer tribe that has fully bought into their dream.

We must believe that our dream is not something to come up with and then let just sit there. The entrepreneur knows that a dream can be reached with hard work. The quest to make a difference in the world far outweighs the challenges that will present themselves along the way.

Questions to Take You to the Next Step

1. How would you define your dream?

2. Where could you share your dream more often?

3. What bigger dream, beyond you, do you feel you are a part of?

STRENGTHEN YOUR EXPERTISE

"Being good is making it
look easy, but getting good is never easy."
JEFFREY FRY

Mastery is inspiring, so it is a special experience to work with a health entrepreneur who is dedicated to a particular line of service and focuses all their energy on executing it well. One way to gain a competitive edge is to become exceptionally good at what you do. Most passionate entrepreneurs will sooner or later be approached by others for guidance on how to foster their own growth.

In this chapter, we'll discuss how to develop our expertise, and how to become a recognized expert in our chosen field, carrying the responsibility that often comes with it. We'll discuss how to leverage this professional development to best serve our clients, community partners, and our team over the long haul.

In the tech arena, striking out on your own and working around established entities is expected in order to disrupt and succeed in that landscape. But in healthcare, the large stakeholders are important. Unlike many other entrepreneurs, health entrepreneurs must work with established giants—hospital systems, insurers, and regulators—to ensure the safety and best care practices for the people they serve. You can go to a tech conference and hear a story of how a company grew from zero to a billion dollars in six months, but for the health entrepreneur it is much more about the long game.

The health entrepreneur grows and improves over time, working with individual clients or patients and building slowly through word of mouth, keeping aware of ever-changing policies and regulation, being mindful of changes in the insurance industry and in large organizational structures. The sales cycles can be very long in the health and wellness field; for example, only after seven years of meetings with a large organization did we complete negotiations and book our first billable session.

When my mom used to say, "Patience is a virtue," I never thought I would be repeating that to myself throughout every stage of my career. There's an intense amount of patience required to be an entrepreneur in general, and in healthcare even more so.

In his 2008 book *Outliers: The Story of Success*, Malcolm Gladwell shares his research on what makes people extraordinarily successful. A factor is the number of hours one has practised a certain skill. It takes a minimum of ten thousand hours of practice to fully master a skill—the equivalent of practising two hours a day for almost fourteen years.[1] So, if you're a chef, say, and cooking for eight to ten hours a day, you'll get to ten thousand hours a lot faster. The average health entrepreneur has many skills in different areas, including but not limited to, clinical/technical, customer service, recruiting and retaining of staff, overseeing major projects, finances, problem solving, and visioning. Developing all these skills requires many hours of learning and a lot of practice, which accounts for why successful businesses are never developed overnight or in isolation. It is a process. My hope is that this book helps you move through the process a little easier.

For the majority of my life, I have been uncomfortable with the term *expert*, thinking it was reserved for narcissists and people who feel the need to tell others how smart they are. However, that opinion shifted when, after two decades of working, I heard the term used by a group whose opinion I valued greatly. They were acknowledging me: "Jennifer is an expert at what she does." I paused and allowed myself to feel the phrase. When you receive feedback from those you admire and are recognized for higher competence and proficiency, it feels like being given a greater sense of responsibility. You will become aware of this new status when others begin to approach you, unsolicited, asking for advice, opinions, and support.

Keep Testing

PEOPLE WANT TO work with or buy from the person who is best known for their expertise and knowledge. They will seek you out when they hear you are doing something well. There are steps that can help you get there, and many of these require testing. Keep focused on moving forward, on purpose and with impact. We will not always get it right at first and there will even be times when we make mistakes. We are going to step on people's toes by accident, and sometimes make decisions that are not best for our company, but if we are constantly striving to do better by understanding our industry potential, having the mindset of lifelong learning, striving to do good work, and ensuring we stay open along the way, we will eventually get there.

> "Success seems to be connected
> with action. Successful people keep moving.
> They make mistakes, but they don't quit."
> **CONRAD HILTON**

Since 1991, I have worked to position myself strongly in the Canadian music therapy community—sometimes on purpose and sometimes by seizing opportunities that popped up—but I certainly haven't always done it right. My layers of experience have helped over time: as student, intern, emerging therapist, certified clinician, internship supervisor, business owner, and president of the national association. These positions and learning opportunities have allowed me to see the many layers, successes, and failures within my industry through different lenses. "Not doing it right" happens as a result of the entrepreneur's acquired knowledge, experience, and skills to date. An error in judgment becomes the learning moment for the next time.

There are gaps ready to be filled between successes and failures. The more we address the gaps in our business, the more our expertise will grow. We will open our mind's eye to the bigger picture and the necessary threads that strengthen the full tapestry of our good work.

At times, I've been called a trailblazer. This recognition has provided me the opportunities to support my industry in ways that are very meaningful. Despite the fun that can come with exploring new terrain, I have also had to live in the reality of our current healthcare context. Music therapy is more often in reactive care and not preventative care, and music therapists are not always considered part of the allied health team (perhaps because music is strongly associated with entertainment). Despite having years of professional standards and training, some days I feel I am seeking elusive answers to familiar problems, such as not having full access to patient charts, insurance companies unsure of what category we reside in (music studio or medical office), a person in the hospital elevator seeing my guitar and saying how nice it is that the hospital brings in local musicians. Each of these problems has a single solution: education.

To deepen our network within our own industry, we need to find the best strategies that are sustainable for ourselves and our company. My best suggestion is to keep testing. Like many of you, I have immersed myself in my craft and the many roles I can possess (sometimes all in one day)—technician, manager, and business owner. I have attended daylong workshops and conferences. I have read many journals and articles. I update my business plan at least every six months to remind myself about how I began and where I hope to go. I look at our key performance indicators (cash flow and customer retention) monthly. I've set up Google alerts to bring the latest news that relates to me and my company to my inbox. I have engaged rather than just followed people and organizations on social media networks, by asking questions and sharing information I hope will have some meaning to others. All these actions have helped me stay on top of the latest trends, research, and the language I need to make decisions. I embrace the belief that "opportunity looks a lot like work" and education is the way out of many problems.

Although I have done all of the above, I didn't do it all at the same time. Each course of action is built on the test and trial of the one before it. There is no failure, only feedback. When you set up a Google alert, for example, the response you receive from that one action may or may not be useful. You may make a few attempts and find that what you've pursued is more distracting than helpful and so you move on to something else. Your intention to build your expertise must stay in the foreground. In musical terms: find the music you need among all the noise. When we find something that works, we begin to build the next step.

Find the music you need, among all the noise.

One of my most memorable "next step" opportunities came early in my career. Less than a year after I had started my business, I was asked to join the board of directors of a local health association. It was a group I was interested in because they advocated for a population I wanted to serve more. They were the leading experts at the time. Although my intention was to deepen my knowledge about the population and the language most commonly used, I gained something even more valuable. I was able to observe and learn from their executive director, who is confident yet open, well-informed on the topic she advocated for, and a compassionate and strong communicator. She took time with each board member to ensure we became comfortable in our new knowledge and roles, reminding us of the mission of the association we represented.

At other times, I have felt I needed a mentor but one was not available to me. When I haven't been able to find the right professional, a consistent solution to growing my business has been to stay connected with the world and all the people around me. There have been times when I have opened myself up to incoming information—a social media post, a magazine article, a walk in nature, a talk with a dear friend, or an encounter with a stranger—and have received my greatest guidance and inspiration, at no cost. Through these encounters I found the solutions to problems when I needed them most. If this isn't your experience, you may wish to jump to chapter 6 and take time to connect with a new mindset.

As an entrepreneur, it can be exciting to go it alone and create something independently. However, the reality is that we all have something to learn, always. You may think you know your industry, but you don't know exactly what you should be doing to develop it into a sustainable revenue stream, or you may have a blind spot when it comes to seeing a solution to a problem. In these situations, mentors—both formal and informal—can be helpful. Their support of me, and what I hoped to accomplish, kept pushing me further and helped me stay open to what was next, learning from it and growing my company along the way.

Pursue Lifelong Learning

LEARNING HAS BECOME far more interesting and engaging as I've grown older. My life is enriched by the courses I choose to take, the places I visit, and the people I speak to and ask questions of. Going back to school twenty years after starting my business, to do an MBA, gave me new knowledge to fill some of the gaps that had become apparent over time.

Regular self-assessments can help identify the areas in which we require more learning. For example, I kept encountering the same problem in my company. When we reached a certain size we felt there was room to grow, but every time we did, we noticed a significant drop in profit. It didn't seem to make any sense. When I went back to school, I learned to mitigate the bottlenecks and strengthen our competitive advantage. Being in my own bubble of a company for so many years, I had missed that my challenges were common in business. I also realized that understanding the roots and foundations for such terms and the issues they described would bring with it the inspiration and direction that I desperately needed. By addressing these two areas, and the disparity between them, I began to feel the change we needed and we began to grow again.

Through my new learning, I came to understand how a company like ours, one that is highly personalized, can become more expensive as it gets bigger, especially when revenue is generated per hour. To manage our growth and keep our personalization, we needed more leaders, and this was a cost that our company didn't bill for. We needed to make structural changes. First, we decided to slow down our growth. Community impact doesn't always mean size; it can mean influence. For a time we decreased our marketing and added offerings of training and consulting to the mix, maintaining a small, personalized team. By blending in these revenue streams, we were able to keep growing without necessarily having to increase our human resources.

A note of caution: You may not know what you don't know. Coined in 1999, the Dunning-Kruger effect is a cognitive bias whereby people who are incompetent at something are unable to recognize their own incompetence.[2] It can go even further— those same people who fail to recognize their incompetence may also feel confident about how well they are doing.

Pursue the best learning for you and avoid the Dunning-Kruger effect:

- Pay attention and respond graciously to both solicited and unsolicited feedback. Remain open. Not all feedback will be constructive, but if you hear the same feedback from multiple sources, it may be worth considering.

- Take a course that deals with the issues you are passionate about. Economics was perhaps the most critical course I took as an entrepreneur (and I would like to study it more). Economics addresses how everything works together— government, public, corporations, social needs, policy, regulation, government laws—and in our case for good. Economics is a much wider field than most people perceive it to be.

- Identify the bottlenecks in your company. If you are unable to solve them with system changes, you may need help with the topic. Innovation often requires education.

When you learn new information, take time to think about what you believe and why, and where this new information fits within your existing knowledge and beliefs. Be willing to question all information and research it further. Lifelong learners dig deeper.

Be Good at Your Job

THIS MAY SOUND simple enough, but being good at your job doesn't always come naturally. What makes you fall in love with a certain business? What makes it your favourite coffee shop, supermarket, gas station, airline, repair shop, or hair salon? What keeps you going back? Chances are they are always there when you need them, they are convenient, they are the only place you can get that particular service or product, they have a great atmosphere, the quality is consistent, and their cost matches its value for you. Public perception and reputation are just as important to the health-service business as to any other business. It is crucial that you consistently survey your clients to ensure you are meeting their expectations. Strategies for excelling at your (many) job(s) may include:

- Working hard and acting professionally. No matter what your job, be serious about and focused on what you do, and act professionally in all situations. Professionals are courteous, friendly, ethical, and tactful.

- Expressing a positive attitude and cultivating relationships. Relationships are the crux of any company's culture and success. Never underestimate the power of making direct eye contact that presents as warm and interested.

- Thinking on your feet, problem solving, and *failing faster*, a term often associated with the lean start-up methodology.[3] You'll make mistakes, but know when to cut your losses if something isn't working and swiftly try something new to ensure your time and financial investment are kept to a minimum.

Be part of the solution. Problem solvers are a valuable commodity in every workplace.

Many years ago, I hired a private, community-based speech language pathologist to work with my son, who seemed to be late to speak. I didn't know at the time that she would not only help my son but also change the way I practise my business. Working in the healthcare industry, I knew that assessment and early intervention were key for child development. When she arrived at our home, she carried all the tools of her trade and set herself up in our living room. She spent some time with me first and I remember feeling immediately at ease and comfortable. She then gently shooed me away so she could get to know my son better. She concentrated on establishing a relationship with him and introduced strategies that captivated and engaged him for the duration of his session. It took only three sessions before I noticed significant outcomes from her visits. My son was more confident to speak up and I, as his mom, began to feel more relaxed. I learned how valuable it was to have an expert healthcare professional come into my space with confidence, but also compassion, and most importantly a plan to reach the goals I had hired her to reach. She made it look easy; like many experts do.

Keep Creating

"The creative process is not like a situation where you get struck by a single lightning bolt. You have ongoing discoveries, and there's ongoing creative revelations. Yes, it's really helpful to be marching toward a specific destination, but, along the way, you must allow yourself room for your ideas to blossom, take root, and grow."
CARLTON CUSE

THE PROCESS OF creating gives us an opportunity to share or produce content that secures our expert status. I continue to find new ways to develop interests that I didn't know I had. I've witnessed the flexibility and ease of accessing new creative interests through technology, something that wasn't available to me growing up. My friends, online and in person, inspire me more than ever with their creative pursuits. Witnessing their creations in music, writing, and visual arts has helped propel my own. Generally speaking, creativity is associated with generating ideas—something you need in large supply as you build a business. Here are just a few ideas my friends and colleagues use to exercise their creativity:

- Use music or your favourite art form to motivate and inspire you throughout the week.

- At all times, have near you an idea book, where you can jot down ideas that you want to develop later, perhaps on your blog or through the creative medium of your choice.

- Get outside, walk, meditate, pray, have a bath, or go wherever you find your inspiration. Ease your mind and let imagination flow.

- Brainstorm with colleagues and invite feedback, or hold your own private *Dragon's Den/Shark Tank*, a place where you can pitch your business concepts to a panel of business leaders you admire. Spark your creativity by discussing your mission and how you aim to get there with others.

Choose your channel so it fits your audience. You could, for instance, write blog posts like I did. You could join professional associations at the board level, write newspaper articles, or produce video content. If you're really serious about becoming an expert, try your hand at writing a book or record a podcast. Whatever you choose as your vehicle, the results of your creative output will lead to further promotion of your good work, who you are, and your expertise.

Be Able to Say, "Yes, I Can Help You"

MANY YEARS AGO, on my second day in a city where I would begin my new career, my life took an unexpected and joyous turn. I happened upon a local library. I know that doesn't sound too revolutionary, but you must understand that I had only ever been in school libraries and had never had the experience of going to a city's public library. I remember being surprised by how cheery it was inside and that not everyone was talking quietly like we had been taught to do in school. I was also surprised by how populated the room was, with people of all ages in many of the rows.

A woman with silver hair and a warm smile approached me at the circulation desk. I said something along the lines of, "I just graduated with my music therapy degree and am not sure where to start." She asked me the most critical question any business owner needs to answer: "Who are you hoping to work with?" This was easy. I began to list all the people I looked forward to meeting and, with that, she smiled again and said five magic words, "Yes, I can help you." She advised that I needed "the blue book" and with that she turned around, went behind the desk, and brought out a book with a blue, hard-plastic cover. As she carried it over to me I had no doubt that this was going to be a book as significant as a religious text. She handed it to me and I could almost hear an angelic, "Ahhh!"

She took me through the first couple of pages to explain how the book functioned. It was divided into several categories: services for children, seniors, and people with disabilities. Each page listed an agency, described its program, and provided its primary contact. As this was the pre-Google era, the book proved invaluable, as I needed to learn about these agencies and approach them with my unique service.

Hearing the words "Yes, I can help you" when I was most unsure was so comforting. Today, I pay particular attention to the experts who say these five simple words and then follow through, and if they are not able to help, they confidently say that too, and provide a referral they hope will be useful. A true expert knows what they know, and also what they don't know.

The Health Entrepreneur's Rx: Strengthening Expertise

A DOWNSIDE OF owning your own company, and being one of the experts in your field, or at least striving to be one, is that you may also have the greatest potential to impair your own growth. I know that sounds uncomfortable but, as we have already discussed, to be an expert in your industry often requires a lot of work and trial and error. Your mindset may not always remain positive throughout the lengthy process these lessons can require. You might end up inadvertently sabotaging yourself or your business by putting a lid on an idea or a stop on an action plan. This happens when we begin to lack confidence in our abilities as an effective change agent. You may also worry about the time commitment and the cost to your work-life equilibrium of implementing the successful change.

Be clear about what you offer and how you offer it. This sounds so simple, but by staying within your scope of practice, your clients will see your education and offerings as an expert service. Never hesitate to refer your clients to someone who may serve them better because you are "just not there" yet. Phrase it in such a way that they know you have heard their needs and you have a suggestion. The true professional pairs confidence ("I know what I am doing") with vulnerability ("I might not have all the answers, yet").

Pay attention to unsolicited feedback. A good indication of how you are recognized in your community is by the feedback you organically and randomly hear. Take a moment to think of the most common phrases people use when they talk about you and your business—without you asking them. You can be sure that if you hear something more than once, that feedback is quite accurate. You can also measure the number of times people keep coming back to you. If people hear how helpful you are, your business will grow.

Increase your warmth. If you are not receiving the unsolicited feedback you desire, a growing body of research suggests that the way to lead your organization is to increase your warmth.[4] Warmth seems to quickly build trust and communication, leading to high levels of influence. A nod or a smile can show people that you're pleased to be in their company and attentive to their needs and concerns. By bringing more genuine warmth into your relationships, you will feel more connected, effective, and successful.

As I said at the beginning of this chapter, I have never been quite comfortable with the term *expert*, but I also believe that when people are accessing healthcare services in particular, they should feel like they are always in the company of someone who really knows what they are doing and who wants to be doing it. Remain mindful that building your expertise is a lifelong journey.

Impact Story: Hogeweyk

How Strengthening Your Expertise Can Build a Company That Makes a Real Difference

DEMENTIA HAS BECOME prevalent throughout the world and requires many experts to care for patients and research treatments.

Imagine that you've been diagnosed with dementia. You're in the early stages and have the opportunity to choose how you would like to be cared for while they look for a cure.

Hogeweyk, just outside of Amsterdam, is one of the first villages designed for persons with dementia.[5] At first glance, it looks like any other village, complete with a movie theatre, restaurants, and shops with many apartments surrounding a lovely courtyard.

Hogeweyk is home to 152 people. The community has twenty-three residential units, each shared by six to eight residents. Around-the-clock care is provided by 240 "villagers," who are expertly trained geriatric nurses and caregivers dressed in street clothes. The staff takes care of everything from cooking meals and planning activities to assisting with bathing, personal care, and administering medications. Even the individuals staffing the various village "businesses" are trained in dementia care to help residents go about their day.

Trained therapists regularly work with the residents and are helping to ease behaviours that some residents find disruptive. Results are being collected on a regular basis and indicate a decrease in agitation and aggression.

An expertly designed model and well-trained staff help the residents stay active, something that can be absent in a traditional long-term care environment. How wonderful it would be to see this unique care model catch on in North America.

Strengthening your own expertise may be the single most selfless act you can do. In the moment it may feel as though you are benefitting only yourself, but over time your expertise will be shared throughout your company—and health entrepreneurs know that taking care of their business is the best way to take care of others.

Questions to Take You to the Next Step

1. How would you rate your confidence as an industry leader, on a scale of one to ten?

2. Do people ask you for unsolicited advice pertaining to your unique skills and talents?

3. What three next steps can you do to expand your expertise?

- 3 -

MAXIMIZE
YOUR MESSAGE

"For any movement to gain momentum, it must start
with a small action. This action becomes multiplied
by the masses, and is made tangible when leadership changes
course due to the weight of the movement's voice."

ADAM BRAUN

MARKETING BINDS EVERYTHING we've talked about so far.
It allows you to share your dream, your purpose, and your
expertise that attracts your customer. In marketing any
business, whether for-profit or non-profit, the same principle
applies: be known, be relevant, be liked, be good.

This chapter discusses several guidelines for creating the
right message for your business. You'll learn how to work
through your emotional connections to business—marketing in particular—while developing a meaningful message
and plan that will gain momentum over time and ensure your

service thrives, helping all the people you are meant to help. I'll show you how to perform a SWOT analysis of your business, and create a signature story that will help drive your customers to you.

Many health entrepreneurs have qualms with and questions about marketing. Blending business and health feels uncomfortable for many, and marketing only amplifies that feeling. Much of the discomfort comes from business elements not being immersed in the health entrepreneur's technical training. Business practices and principles are often not integrated into the general education of health-based training. The results are that healthcare professionals who do become private practitioners or small business owners need additional supports if they aim to succeed. The downside is that traditional sales and marketing classes do not completely fit the health entrepreneur's model of patient care.

Another reason health entrepreneurs struggle with marketing is due to the general scorn many people feel toward marketing and advertising. How often have we been disappointed and felt taken advantage of or misled? No health entrepreneur wants their clients or patients to feel this way, especially as a result of their actions. The answer is not to ignore marketing but rather to change our messaging and ensure that it is transparent and authentic.

I have always felt that there is no greater value and importance for the public than to have a clear understanding of the techniques, ethics, and outcomes from the health service they seek to access. Therefore, it is important that the public is well-informed so they can use their insurance and income for the services they want and need. And that knowledge starts with the story you tell about your business.

Begin with a Great Story

I USED TO think that our story would be of a small start-up strengthening an industry. Quickly, I realized that our story would be of a small start-up growing enough to serve our community in a way that mattered (and would hopefully also strengthen an industry).

Purpose-driven marketing is telling your story to a desired audience. This important messaging adds value and gives potential clients the chance to discover services that may be very valuable to them. For most small business owners, creating momentum through messaging and marketing is crucial; for the health-service business, it is vital. It can take tremendous education and time to get products and services moving; once moving, they tend to achieve *momentum*.

The first role of a social-purpose business founder tends to be that of the evangelist. An *evangelist,* a term rebranded in the tech industry, indicates a grassroots teacher who informs, educates, and builds buy-in by exhibiting the passion behind the purpose and setting the standard in a given industry. If the founder gets this crucial step right, they will soon have fellow evangelists alongside them, promoting the cause. In a service-based business, customer service and satisfaction are top priorities. Customer buy-in occurs when you have repeatedly made your customer happy. You are consistently doing great work. Once the customer has tested the service, liked it, and returns for your services time and again, telling others about it along the way, they have been "converted."

The customer is now also an advocate and will go out of their way to tell their business network about your good work and all the reasons why they should use you as a service provider. They will write posts and blogs about your services, link to your website, and talk to everyone they know about you.

Do what you do well, all the time, and you can't help but build momentum for your business.

It does not require an expensive investment to create buzz that has long-lasting results; it is about finding out where your customers hang and then hanging with them there. You might speak in front of them, write guest columns, attend networking events, or use social media groups to share your good work and vision.

Remember the story I told you in the last chapter about the librarian? I was so relieved when I heard her words—"Yes, I can help you"—and even more so when she showed me the very helpful blue book that gave me a list of potential clients to contact. She followed through on her promise and exceeded my expectations. You can bet I told others about the librarian and the resourcefulness she exhibited. If this story happened today, I would have shared it all over my social media accounts so others could benefit as well.

With our messaging, we have an opportunity to educate the market about what it is we do—often something innovative, or a new spin on a known service or business model. Through good marketing and a great story, we can make people curious, give them important information, engage them, and issue a call to action that will appeal to those who would benefit from our services.

Exposure is the first step to people learning about your services and then translating their newfound knowledge into using your services. The best exposure develops over time and builds in momentum. Three considerations support this endeavor: *think long, cast wide, and get niche.*

Think Long

IN PREPARING YOUR marketing strategy, regardless of size, it is critical to start with your ultimate mission. Think of it as the long game. Your marketing must express passion and relentless intensity. Because our aim is always to be sustainable, we must be concerned with seeing where our business will end up in ten years', twenty years', thirty years' time. Longevity is part of momentum and requires staying focused on the client with their current and changing needs.

The word *change* inspires dread in many people. However, when running a business, change is our friend—a need for change indicates a growing business. If we need more employees, there's a change; if we need to expand our business model to scale up effectively, that's another change. In other words, we *want* change in our business.

Lack of momentum can also be attributed to mindset struggles. Taking time to reflect on several tangible strategies can help influence your mindset and redirect it for growth. Here are five messaging strategies that I hope will help you move in the right direction:

1. **Repeatedly clarify your service benefits to your current and potential clients.** Use messaging to share how valuable your service can be and how they can benefit from it in terms of well-being, saving time, accelerating improvement, and so on. It's about getting the client to share their problem with you, and then you share how you can help.

2. **Design the language to be shared.** Your evangelists are your staff and your loyal client partners who have benefitted from your service. Give them the vocabulary to be ambassadors for you and your services; give them relief by solving their problem. Help them with their sell by using the same phrases and scripts again and again, such as "music speaks when words cannot," a memorable slogan that easily comes to mind when the situation calls for it.

3. **Repeatedly feature your signature story.** This step links back to the big dream we talked about in chapter 1. You need to identify your signature story, the one that highlights your mission, the reason you do what you do. I discuss crafting your signature story in the Health Entrepreneur's Rx section in this chapter. In one way or another, share that story in whole or in bits and pieces throughout all your marketing campaigns. Define the feeling you hope your audience takes away with them when they hear your mission. Telling your story feels less like "selling" and is really the best way to communicate with, understand, and know your customers. Your messaging should contain language that will evoke the feelings you want to linger long after using your services.

4. **Recruit and retain your advocates.** In addition to the evangelists I mention above, you need other advocates to spread

the word. "Amplifiers" are people or organizations with a large following in certain circles or on social media. How can you create partnerships and exchanges with them that entice them to help you spread the word? What do they care about that you also care about? Tap into shared ideals and create value for them. Building your database with a strategy to stay in contact is at the heart of your customer growth and retention.

5. **Remove client barriers.** Being accessible and authentic makes it easy for people to contact you. Start by making your contact details easy to find on your website and in social media. Also offer various channels for people to get in touch, for example in person, in writing, or by sending a quick message through social media. We will discuss this step in more detail in chapter 8.

Cast Wide

RECENT RESEARCH SUGGESTS THAT 84 percent of consumers say they either completely or somewhat trust recommendations about products and services from family, colleagues, and friends—making these recommendations the highest-ranked source for trustworthiness.[1] Word of mouth (WOM) matters.

Author Andy Sernovitz shows four easy steps to create WOM buzz:

1. **Be interesting.**
2. **Make it easy.**
3. **Make people happy.**
4. **Earn trust and respect.**[2]

Although it sounds too simple to be true, my experience suggests that this, indeed, is all that it takes. But each of these steps can be difficult to achieve and require a lot of work.

For us, good buzz that started more than twenty-five years ago is still being felt today, and seems to be increasing in its resonance. My husband jokes, "It took you only twenty-five years to become an overnight success." Being consistent with our messaging and sticking it out through the tough times has helped with our WOM referrals and ultimately our community impact. During the tough times, business owners and leaders should be out there casting an even wider net—networking, publishing, speaking, teaching, and constantly sharing the core message. It is also vital that the work itself never loses its quality and value. I am not going to pretend that this is easy, but nothing of lasting value will happen quickly.

Other marketing efforts ideally complement and strengthen WOM, helping people to know how to talk about you and your services. You'll get the best exposure when you deliver your message to your market from many angles. Using only one form of communication is not as effective as casting a wide net, especially for small businesses.

Some vehicles to consider include:

- an interesting and informative website with great search term recognition and easy ways for customers to connect with you, such as a bold "contact me" button;

- social media interactions across all channels where your audience congregates—listening and communicating back and forth generate the greatest buzz online;

- email and video marketing—these direct communications

to customers and prospective clients inform them of all your internal news and successes;

- magazine articles, book chapters, and blog posts (among the best business cards you can present to your future customers);

- networks where your customers hang out, such as conferences, annual general meetings, and online groups;

- presentations to decision makers and to those who will benefit directly from your services and products;

- day-to-day operations—because marketing internally can be just as important as marketing externally and may be the key to your company's momentum. It is perhaps even more important, and more efficient, to have your employees' buy-in (in-house evangelists) as it is making a new customer sale.

Get Niche

CREATING BUZZ FOR music therapy in the early 1990s happened more quickly than I anticipated. I believe success happened in part due to the timing. Being first on the scene, driving public interest, has its advantages; but consistent marketing, recruiting new clients, and retaining the right team have sustained our growth. Face-to-face meetings quickly led to market growth, and we would hire one new full-time staff each year for the first twenty years to keep up with the referrals.

The blue book that I had access to during that fateful visit to the library meant that I could reach the people I wanted to work with. It also taught me the benefit of focusing on one thing. Jim Burns, president of Avitage Consulting, suggests that investing in momentum marketing requires "a customer-centric content strategy."[3] Although we market wide, we are doing so with a narrow niche. A narrow niche or specialty will help you prospect effectively and build momentum as you create a brand. I relentlessly test the effectiveness of our services through customer surveys, and the feedback I often get from customers is to just keep doing what we are doing well: "You do music therapy the very best and the city needs you to do more of it."

You could follow the best health-service practices, but if your service doesn't appeal to your market, your business won't gain traction. A successful health-service business combines the cause with the needs of your target client or patient and offers the services that resonate with those needs and wants. Warby Parker is a shining example of a product that is working in this way. They attract busy, cash-strapped Millennials with quick, stylish, and affordable eyewear options, and with their "buy one, give one" model, which ensures that for every pair of eyeglasses sold, a pair reaches a person in need who cannot afford them.

JB Music Therapy works in a service niche. It was formed to fill a gap in services available to the public. When we branched out beyond music therapy into other products and services, we witnessed a decrease in our customer growth and profits.

> "You gotta keep trying to find your niche
> and trying to fit into whatever slot that's left for
> you or to make one of your own."
> **DOLLY PARTON**

Use Your SWOT

A CORE ELEMENT to every business plan is your SWOT analysis: strengths, weaknesses, opportunities, and threats. The SWOT analysis is where leaders can carefully address and detail the landscape of their business, where they can feel relief, tension, possibility, and pressure all in one place. This spectrum of push, pull, and turn is what will keep your business dynamic and, with the right focus, growing. I have included an example of our SWOT below. When addressing our messaging and making plans, I frequently visit our company's SWOT to help generate momentum authentically.

Momentum can be achieved when you focus on your foundation (strengths), bottlenecks that the team is working through (weaknesses), daily pursuits (opportunities), and when little attention is given to the things you cannot change (threats). At this stage in my career, my biggest strength is that my business is established and well-known in its community; but, at times, that can be its greatest weakness. No one wants to work in, or buy from, a lazy or boring company. So it is a constant balancing act to stay true to our core service and purpose, to continue doing the great work that our clients appreciate so much, and to innovate, stay current, and be relevant—all at the same time.

I was anxious to get past the grassroots stage, which lasted almost a decade. Those days were full of solving, for the first time, problems related to staffing, budgeting, scheduling, customer engagement, and facility management. It included the first hires, new system development, testing services, and working long hours. After a decade, I started to recognize that some of the same problems kept showing up. It was time to solve them for good.

When you become established, a new style of leadership emerges, one that incorporates greater patience, reflection, weighing the past and the present, and seeking the best opportunities with the best benefit for the company. This stage is a relief after the many moments of sheer panic, impulse decisions, and constant wondering whether you can learn everything you need to know. Important note: you will.

Although this is a natural progression, a sign of the organization maturing, there have been many times I have shaken it up a little, to bring back that spirit of the earliest days. It is often in reviewing our SWOT analysis that the feelings of optimism and hope I had at the beginning surge. When reviewing our SWOT, I become reacquainted with possible next steps, ideas we can test, places we can take a risk and challenge our foundation a little—it feels like playing, and through the SWOT analysis, I can inject some of the fun back into my business. Here is a sample of our business playground:

STRENGTHS	WEAKNESSES
· Brand recognition, reputation, and local presence	· Lack of excess capital to drive growth
· Trained staff and quality of work	· Quality consistency among therapists due to range of experience levels
· Team morale and culture	
· Strong administrative systems	· Competitive compensation to staff
· Facilities	· Driving distances for team
· Positive cash flow	

OPPORTUNITIES	THREATS
· Local market growth	· Change in economy
· Increase revenue through complementary programs, services, and product	· Loss of primary contracts (due to economic downturn)
· Increase local and global partnerships	· Increase in competition

For the emerging or mid-stage health entrepreneur, when documenting the strengths of your business, you may choose to rest on the unsolicited feedback you have received. You may have heard that you are organized, have strong leadership, a great team, consistent services—these are your real strengths, as they are what the public feels. From the leader's perch, along the way, you may add more strengths, such as client longevity, staff retention, and positive cash flow.

Weaknesses are the areas the CEO constantly mitigates and works on. They are the sometimes short-lived, sometimes pervasive bottlenecks. A plan is required to decrease the impact these weaknesses have on your business. Our greatest weakness continues to be the logistics pertaining to our human resources: recruiting, training, retaining, celebrating, and ensuring impending staff changes do not harm cash flow. The ultimate goal is to convert every weakness into a strength. If your weakness is keeping on top of accounts receivables, you may decide to hire a bookkeeper for a few hours every month to ensure outstanding invoices are collected. Your weakness of outstanding receivables may then turn into "strong financial systems."

Our biggest opportunities right now can be found within our client list. As I am sure you have heard time and again, it is best to target the low-hanging fruit—for us that means our current clients with whom we already have a relationship, which we would like to deepen. We can do this by increasing our number of sessions, increasing the numbers of individuals we see each week, adding in a consultation element for larger projects, or providing workshops that support an agency's bigger aims (in other words, staff education). Bringing opportunities to fruition means greater impact.

What I would consider our biggest threat—and you've probably felt this too—is the economy. When there's a downward turn in the economy, we feel it because we are predominately serving the public sector or people using disposable dollars to pay for our private healthcare services. A lot of the money that comes to us is through our healthcare partners (where we provide service) and their fundraising efforts. When an economic downturn strikes, funding becomes more difficult for them.

During the last recession, and during the few before that (we've been around a while), it became more important for me to find a way to make our revenue stream viable and maintain positive cash flow. So far, we have managed to make it work—some would say against the odds. We do so by staying broad in the scope of the work and narrow in our service niche. We increase our marketing budget and make sure our team has all the supports they require to do their best work.

Amplify Your Message

NOW THAT WE'VE done a little bit of pre-work, and begun to see a few gaps we can fill, it's time to get down to our marketing plan—keeping in mind that we are ultimately sending out a message that serves to tell and spread our story, to make people understand and engage with our purpose. The tricky part is finding out what marketing strategies work best for your clients, your targeted audience. Besides trusting your gut and doing some market research, you're going to achieve this through trial and error. Each of our businesses is unique, and we are all in unique communities.

Lisa Sasevich, a.k.a. the queen of sales conversion, recommends an exercise that helps us identify our unique offer: imagine your ideal client walking away from an interaction with you completely satisfied.[4] In the evening, when they are lying in bed with their spouse, talking about their day, how would they describe what they got out of the interaction with you?

Try this exercise yourself. Grab a journal and a pen (or download *Wellness Incorporated: The Health Entrepreneur's Workbook*), and imagine your ideal client and what they would say about you. Now think about what they would have missed if they hadn't met you or benefitted from your service or product. What would be different in their life at this point? What would they be missing or lacking? Finally, think about how they benefited from the interaction.

Just write down the answers without thinking—no filters, let it flow. Once you have it all down, go over your writing and underline useful words and phrases. This exercise helps you clarify what you're offering, what your differentiators are, and how to convey that in everyday language without sounding "salesy."

You need to collect the right quantifiable data, but you also need to trust your instincts, along with your previous experience of recognizing the indicators that equate to success. You need to have a good conversation with yourself and say, "Is this one working?"

Your marketing plan needs to be just as simple as your business plan, something you refer to and use regularly. My ultimate goal and what I want out of our marketing plan is essentially two to five small agency or individual referrals a month and/or two to three large agency referrals a year—that is our benchmark and fits our slow-growth yet sustainable business model. When we reach these targets, we know our marketing plan is working. To get these agency inquiries each month with the aim of converting at least one of them into a client, we have a marketing plan that looks something like this:

- Our team needs to be healthy (not taking too many sick days), prepared (weekly Monday morning training), and provide the desired outcomes (reaching client goals) every time.

- Our company will send out a personalized message, notice of upcoming events, or information that is important to our clients with every invoice.

- Our company will generate a monthly e-newsletter linking to a new or updated blog post that is pertinent to our clients.

- Our company will submit articles to two to four online or print magazines a year.

- I, as the owner, or one of our management team will present our company story at least once a month to our target audiences through keynotes, videos, classroom visits, and so on.

Showcase Your Services

HERE ARE A few marketing strategies that I have found can greatly showcase your services and enhance community impact. You are probably familiar with them already; the question is, are you implementing them?

- **Be a member.** Join your industry's associations and others that support your business. Jot down all the groups that you do or could belong to and that would support your skill development or business growth, including associations directly related to your industry, research groups, the chamber of commerce, and other networking groups where you feel you would experience meaningful interactions. When I was part of several groups, not always at the same time, I found myself entering into some surprising opportunities.

- **Join a board.** Being on the board of my industry's national association earned me quotes in some of our largest national magazines. Being part of a regional or national board gave me deeper insights into our industry and also helped me shape some of the policies behind our work. Participating in research groups gave me access to cutting-edge research findings that then contributed to our day-to-day operations. Joining business groups gave me the support I needed as a leader in healthcare. Staying involved at these higher levels opens doors and also leads to many meaningful friendships with like minds. I am also trying to help other entrepreneurs start and implement their business dream in a deeper way. I strategically volunteer as a board member of the Famous 5 Foundation, a group dedicated to helping young female leaders rise up. By being on the board, I again learn new leadership language from a variety of industries all working toward a singular mission.

- **Volunteer.** Volunteering is a cost-effective and meaningful way to learn about deeper issues and needs in my community and to contribute at the same time. One area I was very interested in when I first started my practice was neuro-rehabilitation. I wanted eventually to work with people who had sustained severe head injuries, but frankly, I didn't know the recovery research, language, nor best techniques for healing this population. So it made sense to approach our regional brain injury society about volunteering. I learned much and was surprised by the impact my newly acquired knowledge had on the growth of my business for the next two decades.

- **Express it.** Putting together a live presentation that highlights your business story and the outcomes of your services can often be the most direct way to a new contract. You can showcase your services, and more importantly your brand, through these in-services (short educational presentations to key stakeholders), using videos, blogs, and specific events that reach your target audience. In this way, you add value and provide a small "taster" of what you do to many people. It is also a way to hone your message and learn how to effectively convey it. Using in-services also creates a localized buzz when your audience at an agency begins to speak to your message, hopefully leading to positive decision making at the upper levels.

- **Speak up.** Placing yourself in a position where you have to listen a lot and talk only when you have something relevant to say is a great exercise for anyone—but especially for the business owner. Meetings that relate to your target audience are another way to immerse yourself in the needs and language of the clients you serve. These are not meetings for meetings' sake but are instead a way we can learn and contribute to the needs of our clients.

- **Engage on social media.** Being present on social media is one thing; being engaged is another. I have heard several people say, "Don't put your business on any of these platforms unless you plan to communicate with those that want to learn more about you." They have a point. When we are active there, social media works really well for engaging our team, retaining our clients, and attracting new ones. Activity on social media means commenting on other people's blogs and posts, all while thoughtfully conveying your expertise in every response. Being consistent is by far the best way to increase your accessibility and to maximize the potential of this relatively free platform—not to mention the platform algorithms respond best when you are a regular visitor and contributor. It is also a great way to celebrate the work of others who are growing your industry alongside you.

Regardless of which marketing tools you choose, the best marketing message is always based on your personal signature stories, the central raison d'être of your organization, and it conveys it loud and clear through your logo, your posts, and your interactions with existing and potential clients.

The ideal marketing mix is unique to each business and location. Find yours and your business will thrive.

The Health Entrepreneur's Rx: Design Your Signature Story

THROUGH THE HEALTH entrepreneur's lens, building momentum can be far more important than growing profits (although these will follow). When tough times strike and you are headed downhill, momentum comes easy; building upward momentum can feel far more difficult. However, the reward brings with it a sense of energy that fosters larger contributions to something greater than yourself.

Successful messaging is most often entertaining and engaging. One of the best ways I've learned to be compelling is to go one step beyond the single-sentence description, which you definitely need for your marketing, and into the more robust signature story. You may have a few signature stories, in other words, examples of how your services have best benefited others. Developing your signature stories can be incredibly powerful and moving experiences for your staff as well as clients. Turn that one sentence into something much bigger, significantly more emotionally engaging and thus memorable. Share the details that make a story come alive: plot, characters, setting, and tension.

Think of the spark that led to the big dream as the beginning and end points. The story is all about the in-between:

what drives us, what sustains us, and what makes our work meaningful as we stride purposefully from A to B. My signature story is deeply personal:

One Friday, at Grandad's long-term care hospital, my granny walked over to me, gave me a hug, and handed me a piece of music. "Jenny, I brought this sheet music from home. It is Grandad's favourite song. Would you please learn it and sing it to him next week?" It seemed like such an odd request. Grandad had recently been placed in long-term care after a massive stroke and could no longer speak, let alone sing. With some reluctance I said, "Sure." It was confusing to see him there with others who were experiencing such changes in their health—from patients who seemingly just wandered the halls for no reason to others who would call out to me to come closer.

I arrived the following Friday with my guitar in hand. Granny pulled up a chair beside the bed where Grandad was resting, leaned down, and said into his ear, "I've asked Jenny to sing a song you like."

Granny put her hand on my shoulder and said, "Go ahead, dear." I felt nervous and looked down at the lyrics resting on my lap. After a moment, I began to sing a song written many years before I was born.

I noticed a change in the sounds around me. The typical commotion and loud conversations in the hallways stopped. Although my back was to the door, I could tell that some people were beginning to look in. One of the wandering patients came right into Grandad's room, stood beside me, and Granny offered him a chair. It surprised me when this new guest started to sing the words that, to me, were still new, a World War II classic. Even the woman who regularly yelled in the hallways stood behind me and began to sing. I had no idea so many people knew this song. Granny smiled and said, "Keep going, dear."

I finished the song and looked up from the words into Grandad's eyes. He was crying. He reached out for my hand and squeezed it. It was the first time I felt any real connection to Grandad. I looked around the room and knew something bigger than me was happening that I couldn't yet describe.

Granny rested her hand on my shoulder and announced proudly to the room, "Jenny will be here to sing every Friday night." I smiled.[5]

Although I couldn't describe what was going on, I knew the moment was important. I also had my signature story, my detailed "why"—even though I may not have realized it at the time. You may feel you have many signature stories that have taken you to launching your health business. Our signature stories speak to our values, our purpose. They express the reason why we do what we do. At the same time, they represent what we do, how we do it, the feeling we have about it, and what we believe people are going to get out of it. It is how people learn about us, know how to access us, and ultimately why people want to engage in our dream and services.

How do you know if you have achieved marketing momentum? You are getting regular referrals, unsolicited positive feedback, and more followers than you have gone looking for. You may even be testing ideas or expanding your scope of practice, and people are buying in quickly because they believe in you. By thinking about the big picture, casting a wide marketing net, and effectively articulating the story of your mission to your core niche, your health service business will make an impact in your community.

Impact Story: Toyota Research Institute

Create a Message That Means
Something to Your New and Existing Clients

JIM ADLER, VICE president at Toyota Research Institute (TRI), says he is playing the "long game" as he focuses all their energy on helping TRI, the market leader for robotics. Adler told *Marketing Week*: "More and more robots are going to become part of our world, that's just a reality. The big challenge will be finding market adoption." Their message's ultimate goal is to help marginalized groups and, as he says, add the "e" after "car" (care).[6]

"This sentiment reflects one of Toyota's core values," says Doug Moore, senior manager of Future Mobility Business and Technology for Human Support. He goes on to say that "in order to provide continual improvement you need to know the stories behind the people you are serving and what their explicit needs are." The customer's needs are what guide Toyota's innovations.[7]

At the root of all communications is Toyota's social mission—to ensure quality of life for all. Throughout the 2018 Winter Olympics, Toyota repeatedly shared footage of their robots designed to help people with limited mobility, including the elderly and chronically ill. The robot, which Toyota calls a Human Support Robot, stands a little over four feet tall. It has one arm with a gripper; instead of legs, it roves around flat surfaces on a wheeled base. The robot can be called with a touchscreen controller.

Toyota has already put robots to work in Japanese hospitals and homes of war veterans who have suffered significant injuries. Japan has one of the largest aging populations in the world, with over a quarter of its 127 million people over the age of six-ty-five, according to 2015 data from The World Bank.[8] This very large group is part of the motivation behind Toyota working on robots to help people maintain and even gain a higher level of independence and quality of life.

When it comes to having a meaningful message that you can't ignore, Toyota seems to have it all: proven technology, social innovation, and car(e)ing values fully expressed to ensure quality of life for all.

Questions to Take You to the Next Step

1. Does your SWOT analysis reveal an accurate story of your business and show the gaps you need to work on to develop a stronger message?

2. What have you identified as your signature story?

3. Are you confident that your current clients and staff know your primary message and are sharing it in a way that is creating momentum?

– 4 –

SCALE FOR IMPACT

―――――――――

"Everyone wants to live on top of
the mountain, but all the happiness and growth
occurs while you're climbing it."
ANDY ROONEY

WHAT CONTINUES TO be a challenge for all emerging entrepreneurs, whether service-based or product-based, is the
critical factor of scaling their business to achieve their
desired community impact.

This chapter will help you fill in some of the gaps that
you may be missing *before* you scale, ensuring the necessary
foundation is set to endure the upcoming growth—and live
through the occasional struggles your business will encounter
as it strives to get there.

Even at the best of times, as we make what works for one
customer work for so many more, scaling can be one of the
most challenging aspects of a leader's job. Here's when you'll
know that scaling is happening or about to happen:

- You work with one agency and they want more service hours from you.

- You have received many referrals.

- You are presented with a new project that requires you to be in a role that supervises a larger team and will need greater organizational management skills as well as your technical expertise.

- Another city has requested you bring your services to their area once a week.

- Your customer schedule has completely filled and you have a waiting list for your services.

- You have more clients than you can manage and are becoming concerned that quality is being sacrificed.

Growing a company will look different for everyone—for some it may be hiring your first employee, and for others it may be tripling your customer base.

Regardless of where you are in your business's development, scaling needs to be a critical part of your strategy in order to avoid what scaling can really do best: magnify your weaknesses.

Scaling emphasizes the gaps and obstacles that are in and around your business. That is why, hands-down, this is the chapter I struggled with the most. I consider scaling to be the most important skill I needed to develop to make a difference with my company. Finding the scaling strategies that work for you may take some testing, but from my experience it is worth it.

Make Small, Incremental Steps

ONE OF THE reasons people think that scaling a service-based business can be so difficult is because entrepreneurs naturally dream big. There is a paradoxical quality to scaling—the health entrepreneur sees the end result, something bigger contributing to something greater, but there are so many little steps required to get there. To realize their dream, health entrepreneurs must do what many of them are not so good at: the small, day-to-day operations that keep the business moving.

A vision compels us to grow our company to a size that will allow it to optimally serve its purpose. Although that size is going to be different for every organization, the requirements to get there are very similar.

There are many reasons why people choose to scale. For my business, I felt I had no choice.

I wish I could tell you that I had outlined the scaling of my business in a well-detailed business plan with mindfully set milestones and deadlines. In some ways, I was pushed into it long before I was ready, but would we have scaled any other way? That is why I believe in trusting the moments that are dealt to us, for even the most uncomfortable ones can be part of our growth, transformation, and development.

I had been a private practitioner for almost two years and had been full to capacity for several months when I learned I was pregnant with my first child. Up to that moment, scaling my business meant building my portfolio so I had a full case-load and could pay my rent and monthly expenses. Learning I was pregnant brought in some new questions, such as, "How will I work when I have a baby?" followed by my clients asking, "Who will be covering for you when you are away?" I needed to prepare for scaling right away.

I had never wanted to grow to be a huge firm in a large corporate office, but I did want to serve many more people in my community, and for that I needed a team. Becoming pregnant clarified that all too quickly. I also felt I had a few leadership skills that needed attention and that would require mentoring. Fortunately, a local college had just started our city's first peer business mentoring program where emerging entrepreneurs could meet with experienced entrepreneurs and ask for advice on a private consultation basis. As luck would have it, I had a great meeting with my first business mentor. The advice I received gave me the basic footing I needed to hire my first staff member. Looking back, I could, and should, have done so much more to prepare. My first piece of advice for anyone planning to scale is to connect with a great coach or mentor to help you develop your scaling strategy, someone who has scaled before and had some success.

Carole Mahoney, founder of Unbound Growth, recommends that you ask yourself, "Why do I want to scale my business? And what does scale mean to me?"[1] She suggests that if you can't answer these questions, don't do anything. Since it is hard to scale a service-based business at the best of times, your likelihood of success is statistically rather low when the motivation for scaling is not clear.

As I began to dream big in those early years, I started to get a clearer picture of why I wanted to scale. Our service was already beginning to make a difference in people's lives. What would happen if we could do even more of that? I was beginning to feel that being part of something greater than myself was purposeful. I also realized that I didn't want to always work alone. Working alongside others who had a passion for the service we provide continues to inspire me to try harder, do better, and be open to new challenges. Little did I know that together we would eventually become a business that would have a legacy in our city, creating jobs and impact that will hopefully last long after I retire. I discuss this legacy in more depth in chapter 9.

However, scaling also brought many pain points. I was taught repeatedly through our growth that regular sales were vital, but so was excellent customer service. But these two areas were often in conflict with each other. When we grew too fast, our services suffered, and when we focused on our customer service, our profits would stall. Excellent customer service required more trained workers, more monitoring of systems, and more rigorous time devoted to ongoing training.

I faced other challenges, especially in the early days, including:

- being the first on the scene to offer my specific service (and thus having to explain it);

- having limited (if any) access to cash or capital;

- having no access to grants due to being a for-purpose, for-profit business model;

- waiting a long time for new clients (because of budget approval processes in the public healthcare model);

- being a for-profit model serving almost entirely non-profits;

- enduring economic downturns;

- identifying and competing for the right and best resources and talent.

Perhaps you can relate to some or all of these challenges, and perhaps there are others you could add. Unlike many businesses, a small, service-based health company like ours does not require a lot of start-up funds. However, the "a dollar made, a dollar spent" approach can be difficult when you want or need to scale. When building your clientele, you need to ensure that you have the resources to serve it.

While every reader may not be planning to expand their business by adding more employees or tripling their customer base, *all* businesses have the potential, and responsibility, to keep growing in some capacity. If you are not growing wider, you may be growing deeper: improving your systems, increasing your annual return and investing in the future of your company, curating your services into one niche area, or outsourcing administrative duties to allow more time for you to be the technician you desire to be. Growth is a mindset, and in addition to being optimistic, every health entrepreneur should aim to advance their business in some capacity.

Scaling a health-service business is all about the people and the systems it is working in. Scaling is taking what is inside you, the leader—your goals, values, and desires for your company—and creating a channel to express them outwardly, creating the desired amount of impact in their wake.

Grow, Even through Tough Times

PUTTING TOGETHER A growth plan is easier to do when you review your current business model and visualize how your services can most effectively be replicated.

We are a mobile service in order to best access our clientele. (We commute a lot.) While we have a combination of employees and contractors who practise our service model in the community, every session is unique to the client being served (community-based). We offer frequent service (weekly sessions) and intense offerings (one-on-one music therapy). We chose this high-cost, slow-growing model because we feel it best serves our ultimate mission.

Your business model details how your organization creates and provides value for the customer or client; it outlines your value proposition, specific business processes, infrastructure, customer acquisition strategies, and intended customer segments. Business models come in various forms that include direct sales, franchise, freemium, and subscription models, as well as a wide variety of tailor-made business models.

Regardless of which model you choose, only by matching your model to the most useful systems will you create the flow required to reach your detailed goals.

Before, during, or after I scale (either up or down, depending on the need) I have to adjust systems that keep the mission intact. During these times I can most easily get distracted from the mission and become more focused on the problems. So how do we keep everyone's focus on the mission even through a tough time? The answer lies in ensuring your mission is the foundation for every strategy—this is necessary for any effective strategy. When things went wrong, I never used to say it was a people problem; it was always a systems problem. Today, I feel that if something goes amiss, it's less a systems problem and more a foundational problem, putting the onus right back on me and my ability to make every stakeholder share the mission.

A very helpful tool for clarifying your business model is the Business Model Canvas. This one-page tool gives you the opportunity to put your whole business model on one page and see the connections between the different aspects and how they interact with one another. You can learn how to use it in a few minutes. If you really want to delve into the subject, *Business Model Generation* by Alexander Osterwalder and Yves Pigneur is the official in-depth guide to fully utilizing the business model canvas.[2]

In a recent economic downturn, we lost a large client and a couple of small ones. If I had stayed focused on the problem (losing clients), I could easily have become stuck and perhaps felt anxious. When I left the language of the "problem" behind and instead looked more deeply at our mission to "provide excellent services that transform lives," a creative approach to solving the problem presented itself. It was a simple yet profound change.

We moved from monthly team meetings to weekly team trainings every Monday. Although each week we lost an hour during which we could have served clients (which seemed a little counterintuitive when we were losing clients), we used the time to deepen our focus on expert services, team culture, and working through the downturn.

During our weekly team trainings, we:

- shared ideas and new techniques with one another;

- reviewed the latest research in our field and how it applied to specific placements;

- discussed new ways to expand our work, often giving the management team immediate sales opportunities;

- identified challenges with difficult clients (at times, we decided to cease working with some of these clients, leading to new opportunities);

- reviewed many of our company systems, adapting the ones that were not efficient;

- invited expert guests to help us fill some of the gaps in our technical expertise.

More than anything else, these weekly team trainings gave me the opportunity to keep my ear to the ground, closer to our team's problems and successes. I gained the data I needed to fix some inefficiencies and to access new clients based on my staff's recommendations. I also spent time with my team, fuelling my own human need for connection with others.

The end result was that through the downturn, no one was laid off; in fact, we witnessed modest growth. We found ways to maintain positive cash flow, and although there were some months when I was barely breaking even, we came out feeling stronger and more intact. Growth doesn't always mean more people or more profits. In our case, growth meant filling in many gaps, which created a stronger foundation with better-developed systems that led to even better care for our clients.

Hire a Team You Can Rely On

ARE YOU TURNING work down? Not able to start a new project? Not sleeping because you are working fifteen-hour days? Hearing complaints from clients, friends, or family that you are never available? At some point you will need to expand your workforce.

I know that this first step can be very scary. Will I pick the right person? Do I have enough money to do it? Will they make a real difference to my growth? My best advice is: try. If you are thinking about it, you are ready. You know you need this person to grow your business, so try.

Once you do, you won't believe how quickly your business begins to build fresh momentum.

I have always been drawn to the clan culture perhaps because my last name is Buchanan, a Scottish clan dating back to the twelfth century.[3] Clan culture is rooted in collaboration. Members share commonalities and see themselves as part of one big family who are active and involved. Leadership takes the form of mentorship, and the organization is bound by commitments and traditions. The main values are rooted in teamwork, communication, and consensus.

A well-known company built on clan culture is Tom's of Maine, the maker of all-natural hygiene products. To build the brand, founder Tom Chappell focused on building meaningful relationships with employees, customers, suppliers, and the natural environment.[4] This focus makes not only for a good work culture but also a sustainable business model. Organizations like Tom's identify that the most important principle of collaboration is that it can make the world a better place. Collaboration gives employees the opportunity to feel connected to their jobs and one another—they know they're not going it alone. These feelings of connection are known to reduce stress in the workplace and increase employee satisfaction; hence the clan culture may be the perfect environment for a health-service business. I have personally witnessed a direct correlation between clan culture and employee engagement, leading to better customer service and increased profits. In years when we were less connected, the staff turnover was higher, chewing up a lot of resources.

My personal challenge early on was how to promote such a clan culture. Even though it was what I wanted most deeply, it eluded me for many years. I unfairly put the fault of this directly on my shoulders and always felt I had to do a lot on my own. It wasn't because I didn't like working with others but rather because I didn't want to "burden them with the responsibility" of helping me achieve my goals. From an early age, I had a lot of drive and often felt I had to look after myself. My mom worked two jobs, I had no dad at home, and I needed to begin working at twelve to pay for the items I really wanted. I didn't want anyone to feel put upon when they worked for me. This was a big mistake. People, especially those who work in our business, want to feel like meaningful stakeholders, important and purposeful cogs in the mission wheel. By being overly concerned about asking too much of my team, I had inadvertently made them feel as if they weren't valued. They wanted to be more involved, more included.

Here is the phrase I repeated to help me reach the big goal of having a team I could rely on: "Build an inspired internal community (the team) that spills over into the external community (your community impact)."

So it all comes down to hiring the right people and creating an environment they love. How hard can this be? Well, in most cases it is definitely a challenge, but one that is well worth the effort. In his book *Good to Great*, Jim Collins suggests that essentially the first job of management is to "get the right people on the bus, get the wrong people off the bus, and then get the right people into the right seats on the bus."[5] When I consider a potential employee, I hire just as much for attitude, personality, and character as I do for technical skills, and in some ways, I almost put more weight on the attitude and personality. If you select the right people with the right traits, you can train and manage them to do the job well. Especially in the knowledge economy, "culture fit" has become more important, since we need employees to be creative problem solvers and engage in complex tasks—in those respects, environment majorly influences performance.

Author and speaker Brian Tracy reminds us that 95 percent of a company's success is determined by the ability to select the right people in the first place—but we may not get it right every time.[6] In her book *High Performance Relationships*, Jacqueline Peters outlines five building blocks that can help support your team members after you have hired them: creating safety to express opinions freely, structuring clear roles and responsibilities; defining a common purpose; proactively building camaraderie, which can help reduce relationship accidents; and discussing expectations and working agreements that can help prevent and repair conflict when people inevitably have miscommunications and misunderstandings. Attending to these five critical elements can help generate a greater sense of happiness and fulfillment for you and your organization. Engaging our team is the first step to engaging our customers for the long haul.[7]

Being a health entrepreneur has been one of the greatest joys in my life. And creating jobs has been the gift that has allowed our important service to reach more people that we all care about.

These days, unlike the early days, I may not personally know every client that we serve, but I know we have a caring team spilling out into the streets to serve those clients and fulfill our mission.

Bring On New Talent

ON-BOARDING EXPERIENCED THERAPISTS can be expensive. Many therapists have not worked in a community-based model like ours and it takes time to learn the systems needed for a mobile service that serves an array of populations and ages. But the on-boarding program that you use for incoming employees and contract workers can begin with your internship program.

We have had many interns in the past but terminated the program when we felt it became too time-consuming. However, we decided to try again, in a new way. We realized that perhaps we had been looking at internships the wrong way, as time intensive, with little return for us and our business. When we took time to reframe our perspective to look at it optimistically, we saw that we had been missing an opportunity. Not only could we provide newly graduated students with an excellent learning opportunity that would help them prepare for their future endeavours, we could also foster a great experience for our team and our clients.

I asked one of our senior managers, who started as an intern in our company, to take the helm. We reviewed and updated all our previous systems and documentation with a single focus—providing the best possible internship that would lead to a stronger workforce for our clients. Using a new and improved workbook, with a learning language that we hoped would be inspiring, we developed a program we felt would change interns into experienced therapists over nine months. Michael True, the director of Messiah College's Internship Center, says, "The number of internships, paid and non-paid alike, are increasing, which helps students find work experience ... companies are realizing that this is a benefit to them because it's a crop of educated pre-professionals."[8]

For us, the by-product has been creating a means of on-boarding new talent, helping them learn not only the necessary technical skills but also the logistics required to serve a company like ours (mobile, working with diverse populations). At the end of their modestly paid internship, these interns are ready to become employees or feel confident to work in another community setting. Using this model, we have been able to grow stronger and with greater ease.

When it comes to internships, employers have an opportunity to attract talented students by offering a salary or monthly stipend. A paid internship can be an incentive and can also help interns fully commit to their experience; it's also ethical! Keep in mind that various professions have different rules and regulations regarding paid versus unpaid internships.

Entrain Your Team

ENTRAINMENT INVOLVES "MERGING with, or synchronizing to, the pulse of the music." Entrainment is the tendency of two oscillating bodies to lock into phase so that they vibrate in harmony—think of clock pendulums in proximity gradually synching. From a business perspective, entrainment strengthens the entire group to reach the greater goal more effectively. When your team is in harmony, it becomes easier to scale. Entrainment has the potential to resonate with the feelings of the individuals within the group, transform negativity into positivity, and promote a state of liveliness or serenity—depending on what is required in the moment.

What if we, the leader, used this principle in the workplace, in our home, throughout our community? That would mean that our employees would be merging or synchronizing with us, our ideas, our passions. In turn, they would entrain the company's customers. The challenge here, again, rests on the leader. Are you fully exhibiting and living the values you desire to put into the world? These are the characteristics, behaviours, and feelings that you wish for your team. If one of our goals is to entrain our team in preparation to scale, we must first be certain that the leader completely embodies the mission.

To entrain your team to your mission and values, you will first need a strong foundation and a guiding dream (see chapter 1). You and your dream are ultimately what the entire team is learning to entrain to, and what they harmonize with is what will be scaled.

As the leader, it is largely up to you to translate your values and purpose to a culture that guides your team in how they do business for you. Entrainment frees you up to focus on higher-level tasks with confidence that the business is run the way you envision it. In many companies the culture is implicit, but some organizations have set great examples of how to make it explicit—for instance, with a culture code (see chapter 1).

Ideally, culture informs all other aspects of business: whom you recruit, how you treat your customers, when (and maybe even how) you go the extra mile. Employees and contractors should be able to rely on the company's culture to help make decisions.

Another reason for creating a great internal group is that it makes strong leaders who are ready to serve. We often think of our employees as people who follow. But, especially when you're a community-based healthcare service, it's better to create a culture of strong leaders, in which every employee and subcontractor takes ownership of their tasks, represents the brand whenever and wherever they work for you, and inspires loyalty in clients to increase client retention.

A friend of mine who works in a different industry told me she loves to hire people who are smarter than her. She loves to surround herself with people who are better at the job than she feels she could ever be. Releasing the ego is never easy for a driven leader, but by creating strong leaders you strengthen your company as well as the community, effectively spilling out goodness wherever you go. You need to be known for your expertise (see chapter 2) and so do the people who work for you, as their reputation directly affects you, your brand, and your opportunity for growth.

Maintain Positive Cash Flow

CASH FLOW FOR the health entrepreneur is most certainly a critical factor for the business. Many new business owners have asked, "What is cash flow and why is it so important?" The short answer is that cash flow is the total amount of money coming into a business in relation to the total amount going out. If we always have enough money available to pay our bills, then we have positive cash flow. Negative cash flow means that you are paying out more money than you have coming in. Think of it as a water tank: water comes in at the top and drains out the bottom. So to keep your tank nice and full, you need to replenish whatever goes out with fresh water coming in.

I mentioned earlier that one of our strengths is our strong cash flow. This does not mean that we have excess cash for growth; we still see growth, just more slowly than businesses with higher annual profits or excess cash. We don't always have money that we can use to take a risk we might want to take, such as testing a new program, introducing a product to enhance our services, or growing our staff before increasing our services. We still aim to do all these things but are required to move at an incremental rate.

From day one, the most difficult aspect of scaling our particular model has been access to cash when we needed it, especially when we needed to hire new staff to serve a growing customer wait-list. It is difficult to add a full-time salary when margins are slim and you don't yet have full-time work for that new hire. But it is also challenging to make all the sales you need when you don't have the staff to fill the requests—it becomes a Catch-22.

Running a small business with limited capital is undoubtedly a challenge but not impossible. It requires a combination of ingenuity and willingness to think beyond established norms. If you are prepared to do that, you can be successful in building a business that eventually has more than enough capital to function the way you want and need.

Set Your Key
Performance Indicators

LOOK AT EVERY area of your business at all times and "mind the gap," or opportunity for improvement. Keeping track of metrics will help you identify your inefficiencies.

All businesses require metrics, measurements that gauge their growth, strengths, and weaknesses. Mindsets are always followed by actions, and metrics are a good way to ensure your mindset, business values, and actions are in sync. When all are aligned, you will see the evidence throughout your business: unsolicited positive feedback, staff retention, client growth, and profit. For the health entrepreneur, it is also critical to measure community impact—in the case of my company, the number of agencies we serve, how many people we serve in each agency, and the results each individual experiences.

In the service business, it can be more challenging to define metrics—for example, how do you measure improvement in a client's happiness? We need to think several steps ahead to come to the relevant measurable outcome. If the training goes well, then the manager will be more effective. If the manager is more effective, then the team members will be more engaged, which leads to a decrease in turnover. The cause-and-effect chain in the service industry is not clear-cut, but metrics can still give us valuable insights and starting points for investigation.

MEASURING IS WORTH IT.
Capacity Canada highlights that a metrics system to measure the impact of a social venture will ultimately generate social value and lend credibility to any of its marketing efforts.[9]

Metrics help the health entrepreneur clarify what the business is achieving and communicate these accomplishments to potential clients, employees, and other stakeholders. Metrics are also a way for you to assess if you are on track communicating your core values, which should be aligned with the key success factors. Just as with the cycle of cash, you need a constant cycle of information to scale well. You need a method to keep track of ever-changing data.

When I started out, I struggled with metrics, not knowing how important they would become as I scaled from working with one agency to working with well over a hundred today. I was nervous to hire my first employee, and I never once received any financing to help me, regardless of how many banks I visited. Evaluating my day-to-day operations was foreign and something I didn't feel I had time for. Filling these gaps, which often took a change of mindset first, was the best way to fix the kinks that were keeping me from becoming more successful.

It's ironic that most small businesses, which banks, in their advertising, claim to support, usually fail to qualify for a small business loan—especially during the start-up phase. Regardless of the size of your company, remember: no matter what a bank tells you, your business holds value—from creating jobs to contributing to the economy.

We gradually began to study the metrics and apply our findings to our system changes and decisions. Here are a few examples of questions we asked when considering the data:

- How long after the first introduction to our service does it take for a sale to be made? The length of time we've had to wait for budget approval has been anywhere from two minutes to two years. Observing this helped us learn more about the budgetary procedures for our healthcare clients and how we could help accelerate the process (by updating our proposals, ensuring we had the right insurance, inviting the right decision makers to initial meetings).

- How long does it take to place clients with therapists once the sale has been made? Our wait-list grows when we are not able to hire a new employee (low cash reserves) until we are able to provide them a full portfolio (so as to not lose money). We have learned how much this can cost us. Clients do not want to wait. They will quickly go to a competitor if services cannot be provided in a timely fashion. This feedback led to our blend of employees and contractors. Employees retained a sense of dependability and consistency, and contractors filled new sales more efficiently.

- What is the highest price for our services that the public can bear? Our prices were set after a great deal of trial and error. Because we were a new health service, we were also the pacesetters for cost, and this is where our competitors often compete with us. We are dependent on lean margins, and lowering our prices can hurt them. To avoid cutting prices, we strengthen our services and add value. We test prices and make small increases every two to four years. We do all we can not to lose clients when we scale our prices: we give lots of notice for the increase and tell our clients, "If this increase poses undue hardship or means you will be cancelling your weekly services, please contact us." We have been amazed at how infrequently our clients react to these increases. We receive this as feedback that our price increases are reasonable and suit the value our clients feel they are receiving.

Keep in mind that health-service businesses typically have low margins and therefore scale is more difficult to achieve. The early stages of a health-service business are often fuelled by passion, enthusiasm, and the outcomes your clients determine. The challenge is, from the beginning, to devise systems and evaluation tools that can grow with the business and help you scale effectively.

The Health Entrepreneur's Rx:
Scale for Impact

IT'S ALWAYS A challenge to run a small business with limited capital. If you are just starting out, the test is even greater. Limited capital is undoubtedly a big factor in determining how much you can do to meet the needs of your clients. However, having limited funds does not need to be an insurmountable obstacle if you are resourceful and know how to manage certain elements. Keep in mind that businesses on a corporate scale were not the norm before the Industrial Revolution. Hundreds of millions of people throughout history have started and maintained their own small businesses without access to an unending supply of cash. You can do it too.

The profit problem for the health entrepreneur is that most often the health entrepreneur is not thinking about profit when planning the business. Can you be sustainable if people are more important than profit? The short answer is yes. The longer answer is that it depends on how well you have built your company. Tom Dawkins, co-founder and CEO of StartSomeGood, says, "Starting a social enterprise is doing very hard things simultaneously: starting a business and trying to change the world."[10] Without a doubt, regardless of what business you own or its size, both profitability and growth are important for remaining in business. However, no rule book says that profit needs to be the primary goal for any business. Many businesses run a very lean profit margin while making a significant community impact that lasts. A health entrepreneur ensures all stakeholders are happy, including the client at the forefront, the team providing the service, and in some cases their families, partners, vendors, and investors.

The question remains: can you be successful without profit? In order for a business to be sustainable, it needs to generate revenue and have a steady positive cash flow. If it turns a profit, this profit can (and should) be reinvested into the business. Our for-profit health service business can learn a lot from the most successful non-profits and co-ops.

Stick with your core service. In the case of service provision, more is not always better. Concentrating on your niche service and becoming the best at that service will lead to higher referrals and return. You will spend less cash trying to develop new products or services that will only require more resources to maintain. There may also be innovative ways to expand your unique service (for example, offering consultation, group versus individual sessions, and products that will support individuals' goals, or adding an educational component). Adapting your core service delivery can also generate more income.

Maintain strict policies on receivables. Set terms for payment, whether due on delivery, in ten days or in sixty days, depending on your industry and service. It's important that you set policies according to what you need and not necessarily to what your customer desires—and that you stick with the terms. The cash flow of a small business should determine its payment terms. Let your products and services sell your company, not generous payment terms. Although we have a fifteen-day net for our payment terms, we make some exceptions when working with third-party payees (in other words, insurance or government). Often, we have to work within their payment terms. Document these carefully (as easy as setting a calendar reminder) and ensure terms are met. Don't be afraid to follow up with the client or with their accounting department—that's what it's there for.

Talk about your business—a lot. The best form of marketing has always been word of mouth, as discussed in the previous chapter. Always remember that talking about your business is foundational. The company with limited financial resources is best advised to take advantage of this form of marketing by starting the conversation. The more you speak positively and authentically about your business and its outcomes, the greater your reach will be—even when your marketing budget is limited.

Keep your expenses low without sacrificing your service quality. Granted, you need to present a successful image in every area of your business. However, that is not the case in the back office. You may even be able to work fully or partially out of your home. Taking time to assess the real needs of your company, without sacrificing the quality of your work, is the CEO's job. Companies with limited financial resources seem to do best when the office is as lean as possible so that valuable capital can be invested where it is most needed to enhance the customer experience. In our case, we don't sacrifice on human resources and instruments. But we save on our facilities because we are a mobile service. Most of our office furniture was purchased at a steep discount or second-hand.

Keep your staffing as lean as possible. Appointing human capital to get the work done doesn't always require hiring actual staff. Sometimes, hiring full-time staff for all your small business activities can cost a lot of extra money. Outsourcing the things you can't do yourself and paying freelancers for only the projects with which you need help is always an option. We use a blend of freelancers, contractors, and employees, and we take time to evaluate our changing needs at least twice a year. There may be other ways your business can save on the high costs for full-time employees. We have used a phone-answering service, for example. This service may not be suited to all businesses (for example, we receive fewer phone calls now that Facebook messages and email tend to be our primary sources of communication) but having a service 24/7 gives callers a way to hear a live voice and leave a personalized message.

Improving your service delivery, staff training, hours of operation, or facilities—whatever you consider your greatest strengths—will remind customers that you are committed to them and your community, and that you don't plan to go anywhere. Our weaknesses, although they need to be addressed, are often distracting; but building on your strengths is a more efficient way to scale and can empower your company, especially during difficult times. This mindset shift (to be discussed in chapter 6) can often better help eliminate the trouble spots than can targeting them head-on. So when times were tight, we added more team trainings rather than focusing on lost clients because we believed that with a strong team doing great work, we would no longer lose clients.

Impact Story: SoulCycle

Scale Your Business by Creating a Workplace Your Employees Love

WHEN SOULCYCLE'S SOON-TO-BE CEO (she didn't know it at the time) participated in an indoor cycling class, she was struck by the energy and excitement she felt afterward. Her feelings were magnified when she received by messenger a baby onesie with a handwritten note thanking her for attending the class. She was six months pregnant. These feelings made her want to get to know the company better by learning about their values. She eventually wanted to be part of their leadership team.

SoulCycle's hospitality is one example of what makes this company attractive to many people who want to work in the fitness industry. Employees stay because SoulCycle also wants to create a community lifestyle that includes full-time schedules, health benefits, and vacations. SoulCycle implements programs for its employees to fulfill career trajectories, allowing employees to scale up. The staff participates in community impact each year and in SoulCycle's growth plan. When moving the business into a new city, the staff choose a few "fire-starters" and "community builders"—current customers interested in being evangelists for the brand.[11]

Choosing to scale requires focusing on customer service throughout every tier of the organization— striving for client and staff retention at every step. Successful growth happens when every employee, from front line staff to the vice president, feels and enacts the mission in every decision they make. For the health entrepreneur who doesn't want to necessarily grow in quantity, scaling is still relevant. Growth can happen in all directions of a person's business or practice—strengthening technical skills and service specialization.

Questions to Take You to the Next Step

1. Does your current business plan help you determine your next step for growth?

2. What problems or bottlenecks that are inhibiting your growth are you repeatedly railing against?

3. What data do you need to collect to identify your areas for growth?

BUILD IN THE SPIRIT OF EQUITY

"Fairness does not mean everyone gets the same.
Fairness means everyone gets what they need."
RICK RIORDAN, *The Red Pyramid*

EQUITY IS OFTEN what we need to ensure that everyone has equal opportunities to be successful in life. Equality—as well intentioned as its pursuit may be—is often misunderstood as "treating everyone the same" and as such doesn't always benefit the individual in everyday reality.

This chapter is meant to inspire the health entrepreneur to create a culture and environment where everyone feels welcome and equal. Take time to explore your awareness and values around accessibility, equity, and equality, and learn the difference. You will also gain new perspective on how to assess equity gaps and possible solutions to fill them.

My colleague Dr. Cynthia Bruce is a researcher focused on equity issues in inclusive education, in both public and post-secondary settings with a particular focus on disability studies in education.[1] Her passion intrigued me to learn more about the term *equity* and how it's different from *equality*. Equity means everyone has the resources and tools they need to feel equal. Take education, for example; giving the same education to all would be a disservice to most. Gifted students and students with learning difficulties all suffer when they have to follow traditional curriculum. Even among the majority of students, there are significant differences in talent, interests, learning styles, and so on.

Fortunately, more efforts are being made to celebrate uniqueness and build on individual strengths—in other words, treating people equitably, giving each person the opportunity to thrive with their unique attributes, rather than just homogenizing everyone. Both in educational and professional spheres, people are learning to appreciate diversity as something that not only makes life more colourful but also enables us to identify, understand, and tackle a wider range of issues and goals.

When Granny asked me to sing Grandad's favourite song (see the signature story in chapter 3) she was doing exactly that: leveraging a skill that made me feel good (music) and using it as a means to reach the much bigger goal (my connecting with Grandad in a meaningful way). Granny found the equity bridge that would work for Grandad and me together, leading to a renewed relationship that continued to deepen over time.

Early in my career, my client Colleen taught me a major lesson on the importance of equity. Colleen was a highly confident, well-put-together, strong woman who happened to be in a wheelchair due to a serious motor vehicle collision. It was disheartening to learn about all that Colleen could not access in the early 1990s—restaurants, theatres, and even a five-kilometre trip around her own neighbourhood. Since her accident, she had worked as a consultant to help our city become more accessible. She often said, "Until you live in a wheelchair, you don't know what accessibility really means."

What accessibility meant to Colleen, and what it should mean to all of us, is that if an individual wants to go somewhere or do something, access shouldn't be an issue. How successful they are once they take their seat at the respective table may vary from person to person, but the seat should be accessible regardless.

The Dalai Lama uses the term *one-win-everything*, meaning everyone wins—you as the owner, me as your customer or employee, the public, the environment, and the global citizen.[2] When the spirit of equity is infused in every aspect of a company, its impact can be magnified.

Access Bridges as Required

COMMUNITIES AROUND THE globe are increasingly using equitable development approaches to design and build healthy, sustainable, and inclusive neighbourhoods. Agencies are addressing environmental and health challenges while regional and local planners are engaging low-income, minority, and Indigenous leaders in decision making with the aim of creating development that is better for all people.

As a health entrepreneur, you have a unique vantage point from which to excel at providing equitable service. Your business is likely lean and personalized for your clients. Although this model can be more expensive, it means that your community impact can be expanded to include customers who have difficulty with access. There are a few ways that health entrepreneurs can strengthen their equity lens and incorporate it into their business and daily life.

The first step is to discover what your customer feels *they need* to be successful, and how your service or product can help. At the heart of an equitable relationship is a quest for personalized understanding. As you delve deeply into understanding your customer, remember to learn about their strengths, desired goals, what holds meaning for them, and who has influence in their lives. The more you know about what a client feels they need to be successful, the better you will be able to serve them. This can happen through your intake, initial assessments, evaluations, follow-up conversations, and general observation.

A physiotherapist colleague of mine recently had the experience of working with a young client who had sustained a terrible brain trauma and was now fighting a deep bout of depression. The client could talk but her arms and legs were not moving as they once did. She had been in treatment for several weeks but little progress was being noted. When the physiotherapist met her for the first time, he decided to take a fresh approach and ask her what she loved most to do. She loved to ride her bike, and she was good at it, competing in regular races every year. The physiotherapist asked her family to bring her bike to her hospital room. This was risky, because it might highlight what she no longer could do, thereby increasing the gap. But that is not how her brain processed it. The bike, which was familiar, something that evoked the memories of her at her best, gave her just the right motivation to open her hand a little more. First to touch the bike, then to hold the handle bar, then to stand near it, and finally, over time and a few more visits, to sit on the seat. Today, many years later, this client can be found riding her bike with her children on the city's pathways. The bike was the equity bridge she needed.

Equitable care and treatment are different for each client. In our case, some clients feel a very urgent need to recover quickly. For them, we should act as what author and teacher Lisa Delpit describes as "warm demanders," leaders who "expect a great deal of their students [or clients], convince them of their own brilliance, and help them to reach their potential in a disciplined and structured environment."[3] Being a warm demander means you believe in those you have the pleasure to work with and for, and you take a stand for what you know they can accomplish. We have learned this first-hand in setting goals for our clients and looking at the whole person.

In our work, we spend many hours with those who are medically fragile because of a traumatic injury or who are facing a difficult transition in life (for example, a child with a disability moving out of the school system into a group home or someone who has been diagnosed with stage IV cancer and given a few months to live). These conditions are as much a part of their current culture as is the country in which they were born. Ignoring these changes in circumstances would contribute to feelings of alienation that may already be part of the clients' challenges. Validating what they are facing can be critical to their treatment; however, it is ultimately up to them to define themselves, and up to you to listen without prejudice.

In her book *Culturally Responsive Teaching and the Brain*, Zaretta Hammond writes, "Culture, it turns out, is the way every brain makes sense of the world." She goes on to explain that the first step in working successfully across cultures is to "use the neuroscience of trust,"[4] in other words, to engage in trust-building behaviour that will release the hormones that make us feel safe. Feeling safe can happen only when we are not feeling stressed. Since stress tends to interfere with learning, it is important to create an environment that feels safe. The same can be applied to work, creative problem solving, and health care. To create an equitable culture, everyone must feel safe.

In light of this, at times the health entrepreneur may not be equipped to handle every situation and should make a referral to another professional. Ensuring that our client receives the care and support they need, in all areas, is our primary concern. As an example, Lisa Perez Jackson, former administrator of the Environmental Protection Agency, reminds us that "all too often, low-income, minority and Indigenous Americans live in the shadows of the worst pollution, facing disproportionate health impacts and greater obstacles to economic growth in communities that cannot attract businesses and new jobs."[5] Their healthcare needs may be much broader than what we are able to offer, and we feel compelled to refer them to another healthcare provider. A strong network of professionals with a range of expertise and who support one another can build a community that truly serves and, together, helps bridge the equity gaps.

Recognize Equity Gaps within Your Team

AS A LEADER, building on your employees' strengths is another means of practising equity—giving each team member what they respectively need to thrive as well as the opportunity to complement one another. For the introverted person who loves to do research, we wouldn't be doing any favours by giving them a public-speaking opportunity; just as the outgoing and gregarious salesperson would probably feel punished if they were sent to a solitary research lab. To build a strong business, we must be mindful of our employees' skills and talents instead of forcing everyone into the same mould.

Health entrepreneurs may know more than other entrepreneurs how health can greatly impact the wellness of the individual and the team. Because our team is small (fewer than twenty-five people), it is relatively easy for me or one of my managers to have a sense of how everyone is doing, but that doesn't mean we are always privy to such information.

To understand my team's needs, I arrange facetime with them (this can also be done with customers or other stakeholders if you are a smaller private practice). Last year, I decided to do "breakfast with the boss" (a relaxed performance review, with bacon). My agenda was brief: review our history and mission, discuss where we were with reaching our goals, and identify some of the ideas we were working on. I then asked two questions: "What areas in your work/life do you feel you need support in?" and "Is there something I or the company can do to ensure you have those supports in place when you need them?"

Traditional performance reviews can sometimes present as threatening.[6] In this breakfast review, I learned that one of my staff was really struggling with her portfolio. The amount of driving she had to do was causing a tremendous amount of anxiety. We were able to talk through her schedule and make a couple of small changes. She said she immediately felt better.

Another therapist had no idea about our long history and was surprised to learn that we were hosting our fifty-second intern. He asked several questions about our internship program and how he could better support the interns. Another therapist mentioned that she had been in a car accident over the weekend and was feeling financial pressures because of having to fix the vehicle and rent another car. I set her up with a reputable autobody shop that had a courtesy car so she didn't have to worry about the extra expense of a rental car—and I was not worried about any missed sessions with our clients.

As I write these examples, I see the benefits of our breakfasts together, but I also recognize the importance of me remaining professional. As much as I want to demonstrate care for those around me at all times, there are boundaries and considerations for each individual I work with and all the customers I serve. Although equity bridges must be built, not everyone needs or wants to use them. However, the equity bridge must always be accessible—resources, education, an open door, a communications channel, and time with the boss.

Set Equity as a Competitive Advantage

EQUITY IS ABOUT giving people choices. Put another way, these are opportunities, ways that fit with their circumstances, abilities, needs, and preferences—as the old saying goes, "It takes all sorts to make the world go 'round." Rather than think of people as lacking, think of how they complement those around them.

It is through our togetherness that we will find greater meaning and life satisfaction, leading to a much stronger societal and economic fabric.

Meticulon, an IT consulting firm, highlights their competitive advantage as having consultants with autism.[7] Their business model is based on recruiting and training people on the high-functioning end of the autism spectrum and then connecting them with employers looking to fill jobs that require the type of hyper-focus and attention to detail that many people with autism exhibit. Because of their "autism advantage," they are able to provide unprecedented software testing and quality assurance services. Meticulon wants to become known not just for their exceptional consulting services, but also as proponents of social change who strip away societal barriers and create opportunities that lead to better service. They strive to educate the public to see their consultants as having *different* abilities rather than *disabilities*.

Meticulon addresses a persistent problem that can plague many industries at different times: labour shortages. Employing those who are typically underemployed, such as people with autism, can be a competitive advantage and make a significant contribution to the economy.

Katherine Power, vice-president of corporate affairs for Sodexo Canada, said that ever since the company committed to hiring and supporting more people with disabilities, they've seen concrete improvements, such as lower turnover rates, increased client satisfaction, and improved workplace safety. She said, "I'd like to say we're doing it out of the goodness of our hearts because it's the right thing to do, and it is all those things, but that's not what drives a private-sector company to make a decision like this. We're really doing it because it makes total sense from a business perspective and we see that in our results."[8]

Of course, this is just the beginning of the conversation about adding the spirit of equity into any business model. The next step is to review and perhaps innovate your products and services to ensure the customers who desire and need them can access them whenever they want or need them.

The Health Entrepreneur's Rx: Ensure Feelings of Equity on Your Team

BUILDING IN THE spirit of equity in any business ultimately means removing any imbalances where people don't feel equal. The best way I know how to do this is to increase knowledge so that a level of understanding ensures your team feels successful each day.

In chapter 2, I mentioned that you need to pay attention to the Dunning-Kruger effect: you don't know what you don't know. Now that you have realized there are things you don't know, you need to understand that your employees will not know many things either, even if you feel you have told them. If you want a strong company, you need a strong team who feel they have all the resources and tools they require to do their job the way they need to. Knowledge is important but it needs to be *knowledge that a person can absorb,* leading to necessary understanding.

So for you, the health entrepreneur, it is first about recognizing the knowledge gaps and then identifying the best ways to help your team level up where they desire and need to. Create a regular forum, a place where people feel free to express themselves. This may be through weekly team trainings or seasonal workshops or retreats, a time that people can count on coming together, where they feel safe and can home in on specific technical skill- or industry-related knowledge. It may be a more personalized connection than that, such as supervising some of your team more often than others, taking them for coffee and discussing what supports they need in place to do their job successfully, all while imparting what you know to be true and useful in a manner they personally understand.

No two people see a situation, decision, or idea in the same way; however, having a regular forum where everyone has an opportunity to speak up can be a useful tool. What individuals reveal through their questions and comments will indicate where an understanding gap may exist. The health entrepreneur will also take note of who speaks up often, and who does not—potentially identifying another imbalance that needs to be addressed. The health entrepreneur may want to consider phrasing questions differently, having round table discussions, or creating pairs through which individuals have an opportunity to express themselves to just one other person. Not only should these forums be a place to express openly and safely, they should also be a place for everyone to gain more insight into one another, strengthening a culture that values knowledge while minimizing evident gaps.

Impact Story: The Chorus Connection

The Making of a One-Win-Everything Organization

THE CHORUS CONNECTION believes that choir is for everyone. As with most hobbies, joining a choir can have associated costs. With the cost of music sheets, seasonal dues, travel costs, the red scarf or full costume to be worn, plus the time commitment, choir can be quite a financial commitment for members. And most likely, every choir has lost a member or a potential member because that person just couldn't afford to join.

Here are some of the ways the Chorus Connection affects each member, ensuring the choir is fully accessible to anyone who wishes to join them.

Scholarships. At the beginning of every fiscal year, a certain amount of the chorus budget is allocated toward member scholarships. Need-based scholarships can be accessed to cover member dues, costumes, music, and all other choir-related expenses. Examples of those who access these scholarships are students and retired people. All scholarships are handled with confidentiality and care.

Travel passes. Paying for transportation to and from practice can be enough to dissuade someone from joining. So the Chorus Connection works with the local transportation agency to receive discounted or donated travel passes for use by members. If budget allows, they offer an amount to be reimbursed to members or purchase tickets outright for distribution.

Childcare. The cost of care can be very high and can be the biggest barrier for parents who want to come to choir—they don't want to leave their children at home alone or are unable to afford childcare. So the Chorus Connection has created another partnership, this time with the local college's child development program. The students in this program need to intern, in other words, work with children. Through the partnership, the interns get the necessary experience and the choir gets cost-effective on-site childcare for their members' children.

Food at rehearsals. Looking after basic needs such as food can be helpful to some. The choir sought out a local grocer-sponsor to donate fresh produce, day-old items, and food that would otherwise be thrown away. A culture of bringing food has also developed—members who can bring refreshments and food to share.

Tiered membership dues. Membership dues are tiered by self-reported income, helping to subsidize choir dues for the members who need it most.

Tiered concert pricing. The choir also considers the needs of the audience. Providing tiered prices for tickets or donation-only entrance fees helps make choir concerts more accessible for every audience.

Transparency about costs. Transparency about the costs to join the choir is particularly important when recruiting new singers. Every member knows the approximate costs of not only member dues, but all other choir-related expenses, such as music, costumes, and travel, before joining the choir. Knowing upfront can help members plan their budgets ahead of time, relieving a lot of the financial stress.

Management of expectations for volunteer hours. A strong volunteer base runs the choir's operations, from fundraising to ticket sales. The choir considers how volunteering affects those with low income or a family to raise, or who might be working multiple jobs. Not everyone has the time, network, or money to contribute more than they already are by singing in the choir.

Although to the outside world they might be "just" a small community group, the Choir Connection has built some big equity considerations into their organization.

It's possible to start building a bridge of equity today. Each of us is granted opportunities to support and influence every day—through dollars, volunteering, mentoring, or simple acts of kindness.

Questions to Take You to the Next Step

1. Have you noticed any equity gaps in your business life?

2. What can you do to ensure that your clients are treated equitably?

3. Is there an equity gap with your staff and what plan can you put in place to begin building an equity bridge right away?

CLEAR THE PATH

"The real goal of what we're doing
is to have a positive impact on the world."

ED CATMULL

I'VE BEEN THERE—TRAPPED in the feelings of being stuck in a business I have created for myself with the hope of freedom, ease, and fulfillment of purpose. For me, it can take a minute, and sometimes even a few days, before I can shift my focus from how I am being affected by the problem to how to get through the issue and on to the next step.

This chapter was originally the very first of the book and it was difficult for me to move it here. You see, it's devoted to mindset, the frame in which we do everything. Without the right lens to look through, you can put all the systems in place, do all the marketing and advertising, all the service development, but you can still feel stuck. We have reviewed the structural and thoughtful work that goes into our business. This chapter now introduces the importance of clearing the path and finding the frame to do all you can to build your business into the success it is meant to be.

Throughout this book, the terms *mindset, lens, perspective,* and *point of view* have been mentioned repeatedly. The path of mindset is the foundation of everything a health entrepreneur needs to be successful; however, it's quite difficult to express. A person's mindset, their way of being, is not something many of us pay close attention to. It seems to simply exist. But I often feel that the lens through which an entrepreneur looks leads them to success—or not. By paying closer attention to my mindset, I can strengthen, adapt, refine, or sculpt it to find the best point of view from which to make that next step—and perhaps better decisions for me and my company.

In this chapter, you will learn how to assess your own mindset and find the answers you need to help you move your business forward.

Shift Your Mindset

ALMOST THREE DECADES ago, through the windshield of my car, I watched my mom and younger sister standing at the end of our driveway as I pulled away. Mom's cheeks were glistening as she waved goodbye. I had just graduated from university, completed a required internship in music therapy, and with all the wisdom that comes with being almost twenty-one, felt ready to start my own business nearly a thousand kilometres away from my only support system and all the friends I knew.

I'd always believed that if I was happy and just trusted the moment, everything would be fine. I backed out of the driveway feeling excited for what was in front of me. I'd already had a brief taste of living on my own. I'd been employed since I was twelve, working after school, evenings, and in the summer. I learned to value other people's systems in retail, hospitality, and as an administrative assistant. I was excited to embark on a career, follow my passions, and make something of myself.

I knew two things for sure: one, I had a passion for supporting people to get through difficult life transitions; two, people needed help to do that. What I didn't know was how many difficult decisions I was going to have to make personally and professionally while expanding the optimistic perspective that I wanted to live and work in—one that allowed me to believe that everything would turn out okay, even during the tough times.

In my industry, I have been in the role of solo practitioner, supervisor, senior manager, owner, president of the national association, invited guest educator, keynote speaker, and author. I have paid attention to and participated in policy and language development, skill advancement, and national certification. I have slowly but surely built a company that has become a recognized leader in its field. It hasn't always been easy and it's been a lot of work. And, truthfully, I would do it all again—but perhaps in a different way.

I observed an entire industry move from relative obscurity to regularly featured in the media. I witnessed our profession shift from being questioned to becoming a legislated field. I watched music therapists struggle to find work or have trouble launching major projects, partnering with large organizations outside their industry, or witnessing their dream come to reality.

I figured out how best to get our service to the people who needed it most. And throughout, I was faced with making lots of decisions on a daily basis, feeling stuck regularly, and having to adjust my perspective along the way.

There were many days I felt tired (still do), worn out (yep), and worried that I wasn't going to make the right decision (frequently). Although the feelings of "ploughing through" transitioned into "testing and developing well-crafted strategy," the outcomes could still feel the same—and even today I still get stuck and feel frustrated. However, my job as the owner and operator is to position and reposition my mindset to keep the path clear, so I can "keep going," just as my Granny encouraged me to do many years before. By keeping the path clear and continuing to progress, even a little bit every day, I can reach my mission.

Assess Your Perspective

THE CAMBRIDGE DICTIONARY defines mindset as: "A person's way of thinking and their opinions."[1] Mindset determines how you see the world: whether you see the door open or closed, opportunity or threat, positive or negative, glass half full or half empty. It's said that you need to see it to believe it, but the latest science around cognitive bias suggests that you need to believe it to see it.

Before assessing your mindset, know that your point of view is unique to you. As Henry Ford said, "Whether you believe you can, or believe you can't, you're right." We must not assume that others view the image, hear the music, or see a business problem the same way we do. When you and a friend look at the same painting, you may see the joy in it and your friend may see the turmoil. When you listen to a piece of music with little response and your friend gets a little misty-eyed, it just means she's feeling the song differently—even though you are listening to the same piece.

The best thing I've learned to do when stuck is to answer the question "how I am feeling?" The second question I ask is "how do I want to feel?" The space in between often reveals the mindset I need to solve the problem and move forward.

It seems that the choice a person makes is shaped by the options they feel they have. How you view, understand, and feel about the world determines all the small steps, the decisions you make, to get to your final outcome. Taking time to assess where you are and where you hope to be will help you identify next steps.

Dr. Carol Dweck coined the terms *fixed mindset* and *growth mindset*.[2] She believes that to master your mindset, you must first understand that your mindset can be altered. In Dweck's research, the students who believed they could get smarter and that their effort could make them stronger began to show higher achievement—they had a growth mindset. Those who believed they were born with a finite amount of intelligence and ability didn't improve as quickly over time—they had a fixed mindset.

For me, a growth mindset means being optimistic, and such a lens can help us remain in a state of learning and openness to possibilities. We can exercise our optimism muscle by the actions we take, the strategies we use, the questions we ask, the nutrition and sleep habits we develop, and the music we listen to.

Why is this information important? Because when we want to start a business, or when we are working out a significant bottleneck in our company systems, knowing that we can figure it out is the first step to feeling unstuck. Our brain can learn, change, adapt, and help us reach a solution that will be good for us, our team, and our clients.

As health entrepreneurs, adapting our mindset is one of the best ways we can focus on our vision and keep progressing with the work we love. As Dweck suggests, just learning more about the power of our mindset can cause major shifts in how we view ourselves and our lives, giving us greater opportunity to build our businesses more successfully.

Forge Your Own Path

MY FIRST ACCOUNTANT said that the market would never buy into a new "for-profit," unknown healthcare option. Almost thirty years later (and with a new accountant), I have learned that when you focus on things that are bigger than you, more is possible... and if all else fails, there is always at least one person waiting for you at the end of the driveway for a timely hug (thanks, Mom). I have carried this frame of mind with me for most of my life, but is this mindset enough to start and succeed at a new enterprise?

When I started out, all the "social" terms—social enterprise, social-purpose business, social impact—had not yet been coined. Futurpreneur Canada and the Trico Charitable Foundation define a social-purpose business as "the utilization of entrepreneurial principles to organize, mobilize and manage a for-profit business that has a social mission at its core and the goals of creating both economic and social value."[3]

Rather than focusing purely on financial revenue, businesses incorporating this model strive to create "blended value,"[4] defined as a mix of economic, social, and environmental worth. A traditional business entrepreneur measures performance in profit and return for the stakeholders. A social entrepreneur has an additional focus on creating social capital, also known as "impact," one of the key metrics we concentrate on in this book.

 When I wanted to expand my learning, I looked for a graduate degree that would introduce me to the social entrepreneur's lens. I had heard about social entrepreneurism in the news and my Twitter feed but still didn't quite understand what it all meant and how it could help me with my next steps. At school, I learned that the social entrepreneur's lens would inform the mindset I needed in my own business. It shifted my entire focus off the bottom line and onto the top line: our mission and community impact. This was when I began to see that being a health entrepreneur meant I was forging a different path.

Through their unique offerings of new goods and services, social entrepreneurs lean toward innovation with the results being improved quality of life, boosted morale, and greater economic freedom. For example, the low water supply in a freshwater-scarce region will, at times, force people to stop working in order to collect water, affecting their business, productivity, and income. Imagine a new low-cost pump that could fill water containers on demand. This type of innovation would ensure people could focus on their jobs without worrying about meeting their basic needs. The economic outcome would be more time to devote to work, translating into sustainable growth. The focus shifted from the problem (people not working) to the needs of the people (people feeling better when they were working).

Health entrepreneurs have a similar opportunity to forge their own entrepreneurial path and provide their services to those who need them most. Across many sectors, the spirit of entrepreneurship in general is becoming a crucial factor in the development and well-being of societies, with the potential to bring about lower unemployment rates, increased innovation, and a boost in the economy itself. Entrepreneurship, by its very nature, promotes productivity and a healthy economic engine. The health entrepreneur adds another key consideration—their gaze is fixed on the productivity and health of their clients.

Fix Your Gaze

INSTEAD OF STAYING focused on the bottom line, health entrepreneurs must base their decisions on the much bigger, and more important top line: helping others. At JB Music Therapy, our core mission is to improve the lives of people who seek support for mood, motivation, or memory. It has never felt right to focus on the money when meeting these needs. I have always known the importance of money, but it doesn't need to be the primary measuring stick. When your business is strong in all areas—dedicated customer service, great service development, creative and inspired company culture—the money you need to thrive will naturally follow.

Health entrepreneurs have an opportunity to do business in a new way, with their focus on relationships and not transactions. In a company like ours, for example, it is impossible, and wrong, to see our clients as mere transactions. Yes, they pay for every hour of service we provide, and yes, that money goes toward our growth; but their health goals are paramount. The relationship we have with a client often lasts years and organically leads to many more transactions, including referrals. And so, the revenue from each respective client is not something we need to focus on.

At JB Music Therapy, we pay our staff and make a profit like any other successful business. However, our profit margins are often significantly smaller and some years we just break even. Any profits we do make are reinvested in the company; more often than not, these profits are used to purchase much-needed resources or hire more staff. For years, this need to return revenues to the business instead of handing out bonuses made me feel we were not *really* successful, that there was always something missing. This was one of the key areas in which I needed to shift my mindset.

During the early days, I would frequently hear comments such as "If you are not increasing your profit, your business is just a hobby," which just rubbed salt in the wound. By shifting my focus and understanding the true (social) purpose of my health service business, I was also able to change my mindset to one that paid attention to our successes and community impact. The question soon became "Do you need a lot of profit to be sustainable, or does reinvestment in your business, when you have the money, benefit a more long-lasting approach?" This allowed me to forge a new path.

The Health Entrepreneur's Rx:
Clear the Path

YOU WILL READ everything in this book through a certain lens. Mindset shifts can help health entrepreneurs move from feeling stuck to seeing a way forward. I hope to make the case that no matter where you are in this moment—if you're think-ing about starting a business or if you've been running one for twenty years—that you are inspired to assess your mindset, how it is working for you, and if any adjustments are required so the next step can be a bit easier.

In 2008, every news report seemed to indicate that my business was about to go through a tumultuous time, which would affect many of my colleagues, friends, and family. We were about to be hit by the worst recession in my lifetime and the repercussions would last many years.[5] There is nothing like the threat of losing your business to encourage you to dig deep into your values and mindset. These are the only survival tools I really have.

A decade has passed since the first news report of the impending recession and, although we didn't witness as much growth as we had experienced in the decade prior, we made it through... and better than we ever could have hoped. Many factors contribute to the success or struggles in a business—it's a mixture of planning and luck. I found myself reflecting on the earlier years of my business, reminding myself to stay true to our mission and the importance of dedicating time to strengthening our processes in both the good and bad times.

During this time I shifted my mindset to the bigger picture of my place in this world and what my business can contribute to it:

- I cleared the path of the external fears I heard over the radio and online.

- I assessed my mindset, which is now more socially aware and adaptable.

- I adjusted my "living in the moment" approach with an optimistic, strategic, and community-impact mindset that incorporated planning, hard work, and follow-through.

- I shifted my concept of the words *hard work* and changed them into *good work*.

As health entrepreneurs, we will always face change and difficult decisions. When I have had an employee say they were leaving the company so they could "have a bigger piece of the pie," when I bounced a company cheque, when I had a major contract fall through and go to a competitor, when one of my most loyal and senior management staff moved away, fear would creep in, followed by feelings such as "I lack the skills and leadership required to run a business like mine, or any business for that matter"; "I'm never going to be able to make up that lost revenue"; "I'm never going to find another staff as great as they are"; "I'm too tired to make this better."

It's easy to be trapped in these feelings. The cost of not adjusting the lens is being incapable of seeing what is relevant and often right in front of you. You must filter reality through your mindset before making decisions. When faced with solving the same problem over and over again, it feels like your mindset has not shifted and is preventing you from seeing the real issue to solve.

So what can we do when we are feeling the recurrence of these problems? Assess your mindset, then adjust your gaze. If an employee wants to leave for a bigger piece of the pie, then revisit your pie. Come to peace with how you divide the pie, recognize how to make each piece tastier, and verify that your pie is perfectly prepared for those who eat it.

When a company cheque bounces, apologize, fix the immediate problem, and look more deeply into the systems you have in place to ensure it doesn't happen again. Cash flow may be the root of the problem.

When a major contract falls through, inquire about the change and send them a thank-you card for the time you had with them. Let them know your company is not going anywhere and if there is anything in the future you can help them with, you would be delighted to hear from them. Do an internal audit and identify a few reasons (in relation to their reasons) for the shift, pursue your next sale (or six), and cast a wider net.

When your most loyal staff moves away, look at your entire team and ensure you are building leaders in all of them. Support your leaders as they rise up, and get ready for their next step.

During the 2013 Teen Choice Awards, actor Ashton Kutcher said that his number one belief is that "opportunity looks a lot like work."[6] I have come to understand and live by this opinion. To start a business, you work at a capacity that may be entirely new. Also, the opportunities that present themselves are not just lucky breaks, although they can sometimes look like that to the outside observer. In reality, opportunities come from a whole lot of hard work.

The successful end result will look different for every business. Be in a continuous state of learning to embrace the spirit of innovation, and to be open to new perspectives.

The health entrepreneur is in it for the long game. It is not about having the right mindset only during the challenging times; during the good times you need a mindset that is always focused on the good of the company, the good of the work, and the good of what will come ahead. This is the health entrepreneur's mindset.

Impact Story: Fogo Island

What an "Adaptable" Lens Can Make Possible

IN NEWFOUNDLAND, OFF the east coast of Canada, there is an outcropping of rock called Fogo Island. The island has a population of 2,700 and is home to a handful of fishers who, despite declining fisheries, have created a livelihood for their community.

Zita Cobb, a well-known entrepreneur from the region, made it her mission to improve Fogo's economic health and foster what she calls *cultural resiliency*. Through the Shorefast Foundation, which she founded with her brother Anthony Cobb in 2006, she spent more than $10 million of her own money, along with $5 million from the Canadian government and $5 million from the provincial government, to make Fogo Island a destination for artists and the wealthy.

The Shorefast Foundation offers three key initiatives that support this culture: six artist studios; a modern five-star hotel for more affluent tourists to experience the art, take in the landscape, and learn the culture; and a microfinance fund that provides loans to local recipients. One individual used a loan to build greenhouses to extend the growing season, another started a sewing business, and another started a taxi business. Each business was determined to support their local economy, and each had an "adaptable" mindset that helped make it happen.

When the luxury inn reaches a surplus, those funds go back to the foundation and are reinvested in the community. Effectively, Fogo Islanders own the inn through a co-op model. Zita says that the only things she owns on Fogo Island are her car and house.

Any business can be a great tool for an entire community, but not every business is suited to be a cooperative or a social business. In this case, Fogo Islanders have found their blisspoint (discussed in more detail in chapter 8) using charm, culture, and a co-op model to support their community.

As Zita clarifies, "We had everything: this was the most beautiful place on Earth, we were predisposed to hospitality—we've got all of these berries and fish. It was such an obvious thing to do."[7] Perhaps every business has the potential to be a social business—but you need to be open to the possibilities.

The Fogo Island mindset is free of obstacles. Health entrepreneurs work every day with people who have met with barriers; it is their role to help clients break through. A successful entrepreneur is one who can identify their purpose and remove the obstacles toward achieving it.

Questions to Take You to the Next Step

1. How are you feeling in your business right now?

2. How do you want to be feeling?

3. Looking at the space in between these two feelings, what mindset do you feel will help you get closer to where you want to be?

- 7 -

SECURE
YOUR HEALTH

"People more than things have to be restored,
renewed, and revived."

AUDREY HEPBURN

FOR MANY WHO are working toward building a healthcare business, whether as a non-profit organization, a social enterprise, or a for-profit social-purpose business, the idea of self-care evokes mixed feelings, including guilt because of perceived selfishness.

I am convinced that you already know what you need to do to secure your health. I certainly know what I should be doing—but often I don't follow through and do it. I hope this chapter is the boost you need to address the right self-care for you.

Self-care is not an indulgence nor a trendy pastime; it's about adding the right blend of nourishing practices and elements to your day, such as exercise, broccoli, or sunshine, and releasing that which creates chronic tension or external pressure, such as a negative relationship, a money pit, or the uncomfortable chair you always find yourself sitting in. It has to do with taking time to be a human *being* as well as a human *doing*.

Self-care is different to each person and each business. For me, doing my MBA after running my business for twenty years was an act of self-care. After years of trying to figure out this business stuff on my own, school helped me fill the gaps that had been growing over time. My education fixed problems and created ease, allowing me to feel more confident, strong, and well.

For some, self-care may look like a challenge, as it does for my friend Will, who has been competing in body-building tournaments, staying focused through the year on good nutrition, and spending hours at the gym each day despite his cerebral palsy. For others, it may look like learning. And for others still, it will be connected to leisure and spas, be it a vacation with limited phone access or sneaking away from the office for a massage.

Small business owners may want to approach self-care in the same way they approach any other day-to-day operation: by setting targets and strategizing for beneficial outcomes. By turning the desired outcomes into defined goals, the health entrepreneur may more easily find time for the practices they need to achieve them.

How successful we are depends in part on how we define and measure success. As health entrepreneurs we have different success metrics for business—we are more interested in impact than in profit, for example. Maybe we can change our perspective to a more beneficial one when it comes to self-care too.

Let's remember that we can only help others if we help ourselves. If we are unwell or preoccupied with personal problems, then we cannot serve our clients as well as when we are in top form. So make your own well-being a priority—if only so you can serve your purpose better.

Self-care is ultimately what you want and need it to be. In this chapter, I present four examples of possible areas of focus. Do not hesitate to be bold here; for your own sake as well as for your business, pick at least one. Or even all four. You deserve it.

Improve Overall Health for Better Performance

IN 1948, THE World Health Organization (WHO) defined health with a phrase that is still in use today: "Health is a state of complete physical, mental and social well-being and not merely the absence of disease or infirmity."[1] In 1986, the WHO further clarified that health is "a resource for everyday life, not the objective of living."[2] In other words, health is built upon daily self-care.

How can we ensure the well-being of body, mind, and soul? We all have our challenges in life; for a long time, mine was my weight. When I was a child, people would comment on me being too heavy for my age and height. So instead of focusing on a metric of health that would have been meaningful and beneficial to me, I kept focusing on the scale. Only in my early thirties did I discover that putting energy into the fitness and performance of my body was much more beneficial than agonizing over my weight. When I am physically healthy, my mental health and my ability to serve clients in a mobile and time-intensive business improve. When I slip in this area, I remind myself that I can only serve as well as I feel.

Recently, I was listening to a presenter passionately share her message with one hundred people. As the presentation went on, the sound of her breath between sentences through her headset became more and more pronounced. By the end of her performance, she seemed flushed and breathless. As an audience member, I was worried about her. Whether it was extra weight, getting over the flu, or not getting out for a walk in a while, her performance was affected. I felt it, as did others in the audience, and it took away from the message she had worked so hard to convey.

Why is performance important to you as a health entrepreneur? I wonder if we would all answer something like, "Because there is a lot to do and I want to be a leading expert on doing it right for as long as I can." Or, "Especially as a healthcare professional, I want to look after my own health—I want to be a role model to my clients." I want to be ready for what's next and to go with the ebbs and flows that lead me to fulfill my purpose. I need to be healthy to reach that level of performance. That thought led me to join a triathlon team at a time when I couldn't run, didn't know how to swim, and only occasionally rode an old bike. Another story for another time; but the wonderful outcome was feeling enhanced energy at home and at work.

According to a 2001 report by the Council on Foreign Relations, health is linked to political, financial, and social stability. The report suggests that those who are the healthiest contribute to the strength of an entire nation.[3] That can feel like a lot of pressure, but the concept of not just individually benefitting from your good health surely appeals to the health entrepreneur. By prioritizing your own health, you ultimately tell the world that it is a central value to you personally and professionally.

Health encompasses so many aspects, including nutrition, exercise, and freedom from pain. Take a moment to think about which aspect of your health you could improve and how. Create a metric that is meaningful to you, such as having more energy or patience, or being able to walk up three flights of stairs without breaking a sweat. Then treat this goal just like any other business goal. The following sections are broken down into goals you may wish to consider at this stage of your career and life.

Fuel Your Brain

YOUR BRAIN'S VOLUME peaks in your early twenties and gradually declines for the rest of life. A depressing thought, especially as many people begin to notice subtle changes in their memory in their forties, like forgetting a new colleague's name minutes after having been introduced. When you are frustrated by memory loss, keep in mind that you might struggle to remember things as you get older because your brain is so efficient. When the brain sees things that are familiar and unthreatening, it tends to register them as unimportant.

In my years of learning about the brain and how neuroplasticity allows music to affect and change it, I also stumbled upon many other influences that can improve our brain function, such as movement, nutrition, and decreasing the use of pharmaceuticals. Spending as little as ten minutes sitting and visualizing peaceful scenery or listening to music that soothes you has been shown to thicken grey matter, resulting in better memory. Combining time spent in calm, green environments with movement, for example, by walking in nature, causes brain growth.[4]

For Promega, a company dedicated to research that helps diagnose and treat diseases, self-care is not just for the individual but for the entire group. They support their team's wellness with on-the-job "third spaces," where employees can take solitude breaks and meditate in natural light. The health benefits go beyond the individual and have resulted in improved productivity levels for the company.

As health entrepreneurs, developing memory and brain growth allows us to be our best when engaging with people and processing information. Variety is key; we build up a more exact memory if we are exposed to the same information from lots of different perspectives. We entrepreneurs tend to use many different channels for our learning anyway—reaching out, building networks, and putting together a whole picture to find the best solutions and strategies for our businesses.

In my work, I recommend changing up your playlists frequently—using a variety of beats, rhythms, voices, and tempos can give the brain something to work on and strengthen over time. How can you introduce similar changes to an essential part of your workflow or service offering?

When does your brain feel rejuvenated? For me, it is after a relaxing bath or a good sleep. If memory is important to you, you will definitely want to delve deeply into the latest sleep research and the strategies to help you achieve the amount of sleep you need. When you are in deep, slow-wave sleep, your brain goes on working, making sense of what you have experienced during the day. This results in improved learning and memory, while lack of sleep impacts our health, safety, and longevity.[5]

Calm Your Mind

FROM A YOUNG age, we are frequently told to "pay attention." Why does focusing on just one thing matter so much? The moment I am immersed in one thought (such as this sentence I am writing now) or an image, that one thing seems much bigger, clearer, and more significant and meaningful. Although we know that distractions are the greatest anti-focus agents, we still let them happen. It is not my intention to give you solutions but to encourage you to pursue focus—or even mindfulness or meditation—as one of your self-care goals.

In recent decades, more attention has been paid to meditation and mindfulness practices, which have been proven to enhance attention, improve mood, and slow down the aging brain.[6] Learning to quiet the mind and stop the chatter that goes on in our heads much of the time allows us to deal with issues and obstacles more calmly and productively. As Psychologist Kelly McGonigal explains, "When you approach the practice of figuring this stuff out in that way [with a meditative, mindful approach], you start to get images and memories and ideas that are different than if you tried to answer those questions intellectually."[7]

At Vipassana silent retreats, participants are instructed to refrain from any form of interaction, even eye contact, and activities such as reading or writing. One hundred scientists went on such a retreat and noted that shutting off verbalization heightened their awareness in other areas.[8]

A calm brain allows inspiration to take root and creativity to flourish—that's why we're sometimes privy to our best ideas when driving, washing the dishes, or showering. While we're engaged in a routine mechanical task, our minds can explore and solve problems that otherwise have been plaguing us.

As business owners, we are often presented with problems. Our job is to find the pathway through the mud and identify the quickest and most efficient solution. Problem solving takes focus and for that reason we need to be prepared. Professor Jonathan Schooler from UC Santa Barbara suggests, "Daydreaming and boredom seem to be a source for incubation and creative discovery in the brain."[9] I tested this idea when I recently joined a forty-eight-hour retreat that included nature watching and hourly writing. After ten minutes of staring at the treed hills as the sun danced upon them, I could turn to writing with renewed inspiration, not even realizing I had acquired a new idea until it flowed from my fingers.

Create More Ease

THE ENTREPRENEUR FACES several potential threats to their success: project failure, a bad decision, a missed opportunity, and financial issues, to name but a few. Nevertheless, most entrepreneurs tend to be optimistic and hopeful, regardless of the perceived threats.

We have to differentiate between two types of stress: the stress born of an urge to create and the stress stemming from perceived threats or incessant worrying. If we feel an urge to create, to go out there and make a difference in the world, to fulfill our purpose, then the stress born of that is a positive kind of pressure. We need some tension, as it energizes us; however, there are also very destructive kinds of stress. Worrying about one's health or subsistence, for example, can be very stressful. But a lot of "negative stress" is homemade and can be relieved or turned into positive stress by shifting perspectives and looking at life differently.

Health entrepreneurs tend to be good at shifting perspectives, seeing the potential in a situation, remaining optimistic, and moving forward consistently.

Now, don't get me wrong, entrepreneurship is plenty stressful, but I often wonder if some, or many, health entrepreneurs have a natural Zen gene they can call forth when they need it; or perhaps they manage to turn stress from a negative thing into an inspiring one that gives direction for that next step. With that said, there is no doubt that stress can wreak havoc on the mind and body. Researchers have found that chronic psychological stress is associated with the body losing its ability to regulate the inflammatory response, which leads to greater risk of disease.[10] The answers are readily available: good food, exercise, sleep, and medical care. For emotional revitalization, the options of counselling, coaching, a visit with friends or family, keeping a journal, daily meditation, or prayer can create feelings of inspiration, calmness, and groundedness. These acts of revitalization are known to contribute to more ease and less stress.

Nonetheless, perceived stress will be ever-present for the health entrepreneur—there will always be a problem to solve and a success to celebrate. What I suggest is that we adapt our mindset around stress, and instead of trying to get rid of it, lean into it. Leaning in is a coping strategy meant to reflect the feeling that will help you more efficiently learn the lesson being presented. So, for example, let's say you are in a trying situation and you experience an emotion, such as anxiety, anger, sadness, jealousy, or bitterness. Instead of ignoring it, widen your lens to see that life is offering you an opportunity to understand where you're stuck in your growth, where you have more to learn, and where you could focus your attention. By leaning into the emotions and really feeling them, you will be able to explore them and move through them more efficiently. In essence, for a time you feel the emotion more strongly, but it passes more swiftly.

Stress can help us move and grow. When we need to have a difficult conversation, get through performance reviews, leave a toxic relationship, finish an assignment, or graduate a high-maintenance client, stress can motivate action and improve your productivity and efficiencies. In Biosphere 2, an Earth system research facility in Arizona, scientists created what they thought was the perfect environment for trees to thrive in, but the trees didn't do well. The researchers forgot to consider wind. The absence of wind, which would normally put stress on the tree branches and encourage them to be stronger and create deeper roots, caused them to topple right over.[11] In order to be strong, we need to feel some tension over time.

The payoff for managing stress is peace of mind and—perhaps—a longer, healthier life. It may not be possible to avoid disease completely, but doing as much as we can to develop resilience and prepare the body and mind to deal with problems as they arise is a step we can all take.

To be the health entrepreneur I want to be, my health matters not only to me but also to the community I hope to impact.

As health entrepreneurs, we aim to do good and therefore we must also feel good—at least most of the time. The reality is that "feeling good" does not always come naturally or easily, as things come up and life is sometimes very challenging. However, a few preventative measures taken during the up times can create a solid base to fall back on during the down times—similar to building up a savings account in case you fall on difficult times. The following five points may contribute to building your strong foundation:

1. Visit Your Future Self

AS A LEADER, I am responsible for providing the vision, the image of a better future that guides us toward that goal. To sustain my business and myself, I first need to have a clear vision of my future self. This is not always as easy as it may sound. However, to inspire, engage, and motivate myself and others, I need to have a clear idea of my role in this vision and give those who work with me insight to where we are going.

Walter Mischel, the researcher known for the famous marshmallow test, suggests that connecting with your "future you" helps to delay gratification. Mischel's thesis is that those who can delay gratification are more successful than those who need it immediately. He explains, "If you see more continuity between yourself now and yourself in the future, you probably put more value on delayed rewards and less value on immediate rewards and are less impatient than people who view their future selves as strangers."[12] Most people see their future selves as strangers. As business leaders, we must change this perspective and become much more familiar with all aspects of our future self. What will it look like, act like, feel like, and be like?

Don't get too hung up on the details, though—this is a big-picture exercise. As you conjure your future self, rather than imagining the specifics of the services you would provide, picture yourself optimally serving the greater good and the individual client and experiencing the sense of fulfillment that goes along with that. Rather than thinking about whom you would have to know and how often you would contact them, imagine that you are well-connected and maintain meaningful relationships with people who matter to your business and your success, knowing that you are tied into a strong community and network.

The stronger your connection with your future self, the greater your willingness to do the things that will be in your future self's best interest. If you want to be an influential leader, more organized, a more effective communicator, or a stronger negotiator, connecting with your future self can prove to be an important part of an effective strategy.

2. Be Purposeful

PEOPLE WANT TO feel that their work matters and that their contributions achieve something important. Mark Zuckerberg said it best in his 2017 commencement address at Harvard, the school he attended and then quit. He said, "It's not enough to have purpose yourself. You have to create a sense of purpose for others." He went on to express something other Millennials have told me they feel: "My hope was never to build a company, but to make an impact."[13]

As discussed in chapter 1, in a for-purpose business the focus shifts from "just profit" to something else. It wasn't until I began to consider our impact on the people we serve and the community in which we serve them that I determined what the "something else" should be. By focusing on impact, I was better able to define our business partnerships and the goals for our clients and for the company. I could work on the smaller details that would have a stronger impact on those served and on our broader community. This sense of purpose changed the way I did everything, from team meetings to service sessions. Now every step is guided by the intention of making the best possible impact.

3. Build Great Relationships

WHEN I WAS young, I didn't analyze my friendships, but I certainly knew who I liked to hang out with and who I felt good around. The era in which I was raised has influenced my approach to relationships. As a part of Generation X, I am smack dab between the Boomers, who taught me to follow through on my commitments, and the Millennials, who remind me daily to look after my physical and emotional self in order to better serve my higher purpose. I have brought a bit of both of these philosophies into my work.

My business requires me to be a strong advocate for something I couldn't help but believe in—that applying music can change people's lives—but I also know that to influence the larger populations my company services I needed to get to know them, listen to their concerns, and follow through on all my promises, indeed exceed their expectations. Building relationships with clients of all ages is one of the most valuable aspects of our business.

Fran Herman is not only my music therapy mentor but also a magnet for people of all ages and backgrounds. When visiting Fran in her large three-level home downtown, I rarely have a moment absolutely alone with her. Young people rent rooms, and senior members of the family pay visits. Often an intergenerational group with voracious appetites and opinions gathers for meals. The door is always open to all.

Fran makes me feel like a daughter, a colleague, a teacher, and a friend all at the same time. Not once have I ever heard her say, "Well, when I was your age..." or "You will feel different ten years from now." When I am with Fran, I always feel I have something to contribute, and in turn, something to learn. Managers and employees alike have confirmed that these feelings of closeness, trust, and support foster well-being. I am grateful to have experienced this in my own life, with people like Fran who inspire me as I move ahead.

4. Have Courage

BEING A LEADER means having many moments of feeling and being vulnerable. The pressure to lead well, be open, and be trustworthy carries a tremendous amount of responsibility. Brené Brown suggests that even though people commonly equate vulnerability with weakness, being vulnerable is really a sign of courage and strength.[14]

In addition to going back to school in 2013, I was elected president of the Canadian Association for Music Therapists (CAMT). My role as the CAMT president gave me a second testing place for learning outside my own company. I worked on the many questions I had, promoting complete transparency and openness, and choosing courage instead of fear. Although I am still afraid to hurt other people's feelings when I express my viewpoint, I believe voicing opinions is an important part of the leader's role. Speak from your intuition, heart, and experience and then be open and flexible to help the organization move toward its ultimate goal.

Depending on how it's done, confronting someone doesn't necessarily have to hurt their feelings. There is no "right" or "wrong" way of doing things. But, for example, giving feedback can help a person grow or it can seriously decrease their self-confidence. It depends on how feedback is delivered—and, of course, on the intention of the speaker. If an employee or volunteer is not meeting their milestones, we have to have a conversation about that. If I lead the conversation with open questions, then it will feel a lot less like a confrontation and a lot more like an opportunity to connect. I could ask: "How do you feel about your workload? How do you feel about your performance? What is holding you back? What motivates you?" That way we are already on the way to finding a solution.

Having courage will look different to everyone. Some people may need to reconnect to their purpose and dream, and ensure their strategy is aligned with these elements. Others may need to test more often. Not every idea or approach is going to work, but you won't know unless you try it. Create ways of testing things on a small scale rather than going for full implementation straight away.

Look in the mirror and say, "I am allowed to make mistakes." As the leader, your intentions are clear: you want to succeed. Being allowed to make mistakes is a critical factor for building your courage.

5. Find Your Flow

IN ADDITION TO the term *social-purpose business*, which sparked my immediate interest and evoked a sense of belonging, another word that has come to mean just as much to me is *flow*. I had heard this word before, but only in the last decade or so has it reached my consciousness and resonated within my business. Flow has since become incredibly useful during the days I have many details to get through.

Mihaly Csikszentmihalyi is the father of flow. He described flow as the mental state in which a person performing an activity is fully engrossed in a feeling of energized focus, full involvement, and enjoyment in the activity.[15] Discovering this definition immediately transformed the core of my business belief system. It contained all that I held dear as a business owner, a social entrepreneur, a global citizen, and a music therapist—that to be successful and satisfied in work, one must:

- be fully immersed, in other words, understand every aspect of the business;

- have an energized focus, in other words, let all potential distractions fade into the background, feel awake and ready to act;

- feel fully engaged, in other words, give it your all, no half-hearted dabbling;

- enjoy the process, which is often a matter of "flicking a switch in your head" more than anything else.

The Health Entrepreneur's Rx: Secure Health

LET'S FACE IT: life is one huge spectrum, from complete misery to outright joy, and there is no guarantee where you will land from day to day. The pressures of building a business don't just affect the owner but the many relationships tied to the owner, their friends, their partners, and their children. For me it was no different. One of the most agonizing business decisions I made was putting my children in daycare to continue the momentum of building my company. Once they were in daycare, with the most delightful team of care leaders, I had to organize my life so I could drop them off and pick them up on time while also organizing my clients throughout the day. This took a lot of arranging and often felt like a big game of Tetris. The stress of being a business owner also permeated my closest relationship, with my husband James.

During one particularly stressful year (that felt more like six) my husband and I separated. The children were young and I was managing significant business growth that required a heightened amount of dedication. I also added the role of being my profession's national board chair, a move I was certain would help my career and professional learning—and it did. But the cost was huge. That decision led to a nine-month-long, painful separation from my husband. Our separation, and decision not to divorce, meant reprioritizing our relationship to mend the deep-seated wounds we had caused in each other. This took time and a tremendous amount of emotional energy. The outcome was a new life learning that we have worked hard to maintain. I love my business. I love my husband and kids. It isn't so much about balance for me, it is about the importance of the whole of it—the business, my family, my friends, my team—and ensuring I always have enough margin to bend my time to where it is needed most. James and I have just celebrated our twenty-fifth wedding anniversary and our children are thriving in their own lives, remembering to come home for Thanksgiving.

Building a margin is important and can be achieved by incorporating self-care on the days you feel able. Through all my years of working with people who have been blindsided and are facing difficult, unexpected life transitions, I have come to feel that we all need a margin, a space for the unexpected, for random adversity. Your margin may not be needed for you but for someone you care deeply about, giving you extra time in your day so you can spend it with them. As we age, this sandwich generation everyone talks about becomes pronounced. Our parents are aging, frequently at a hospital or needing more home support, and our children are taking up a lot of our available time and energy. Maintaining our margin and using it is a way we can be there for one another. For you, a margin may look like a healthy boundary; or it may be a buffer, such as giving yourself twenty extra minutes to get to your next appointment, or an extra week with an assignment.

The Taoist traditions have actually quantified margin in our life. Bruce Frantzis, a recognized Taoist master, teaches the 70 percent rule as a fundamental principle for all Taoist exercises. First, estimate what 100 percent of your capacity is in terms of range of movement or duration of practice; that is, how far your body can actually stretch and how much your body can endure before it collapses.[16] Once you determine this, you then only move or practise to about 70 percent of your capacity. As I have said of myself many times, when people try to give 100 percent, they often inadvertently go to 110 or 120 percent of their body's maximum capacity, which results in injury, illness, and unnecessary stress. The 70 percent rule allows you to make your body and mind work in a more relaxed, efficient, and healthy manner for a longer duration.

Impact Story: Princess Diana

Make the Changes Necessary
to Keep Doing Good Work

A FEW YEARS back, I drove for three hours to see an exhibit of Princess Diana's dresses. For all intents and purposes, this was meant to be a bit of frivolous fun with friends, having a laugh and a couple of glasses of wine together. After reluctantly paying the astronomical admittance fees to the exhibit, I entered and immediately felt a shift from lightheartedness to something deeper and more sacred. The lights were dim, with brighter lights strategically highlighting the gown and the description of the environment Diana was in when she wore it. But the exhibit went one step further. It told us a little bit about what she was thinking and feeling at the time, in her own words.

It didn't feel quite right to talk too loudly or socialize with my friends. I felt the journey of her life in a much more intimate way than when I had flipped through the tabloids. I almost began to feel her presence. As we entered the last room, which I had been anticipating and feeling nervous to arrive at, I felt an unexpected jolt. This room was like no other that had come before it. It held the flowers, now dried, that had been left outside Buckingham Palace in memoriam. I started to feel the sting of tears.

Moving closer to this final installation, I saw a collection of letters displayed behind glass. Several were authored by Diana, among them a letter that was typed and addressed to more than one hundred charities and foundations.

Diana explained that she would no longer be able to directly support their causes. The stress of all the charitable work she had been doing had led to significant health problems and she could no longer perform as she once had. Diana wrote about how she had to scale back from her work and her passion, for her own mental health. It was clear that she deeply cared about her work, but it had nonetheless become too much.

For the health entrepreneur, self-care is not an emergency response plan, ready to be activated when stress becomes overwhelming and keeps us from our purpose. Instead, healthy self-care is an intentional way of living, in which our values, attitudes, and actions are integrated into our day-to-day moments. It may mean stepping back at times, something difficult for many of us to do but vital if we wish to fulfill our purpose.

Questions to Take You to the Next Step

1. What health issue have you been battling with for most of your life or for a significant amount of time?

2. Could a change in perspective or focusing on a different outcome be beneficial for your health?

3. What mindset shift do you need to make a significant improvement to your well-being?

FIND YOUR BLISSPOINT

"Out of the bliss comes magic,
wonderment and creativity."
MICHAEL JACKSON

WANT TO KEEP your customers and employees coming back for more? Find their bliss. Want to keep being inspired by your business? Find yours.

This chapter introduces the concept of "blisspoint," which I define as the intersection of our values-driven goals. Strengthening each goal will aid the health entrepreneur in easily making their next decision.

A term more commonly used in the formulation of food products, blisspoint is the amount and blend of certain ingredients, such as salt, sweetness, and fat, that creates optimal deliciousness. Finding my organization's blisspoint meant locating the perfect intersection of fulfilling purpose (meeting our mission), organizational health (client and staff retention), and recognized good work (excellent customer service). I coined this intersection our *business blisspoint*, where our values—heart, health, and mastery—are in perfect harmony.

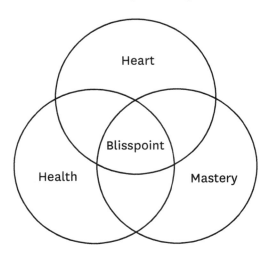

When health entrepreneurs get their blisspoint's proportions right, customers begin to crave our services. In my opinion, it is 100 percent the leader's job to establish the business's values before adding more stakeholders. The expression of these values may change over time, but the values themselves need to remain the cornerstones to the success of your good work.

Choose the Right Values to Blend

DURING WHAT WAS to be a casual visit, a good friend asked me a serious question: "Jen, what would you say is your core value?" I replied with, "For me or for my business?" He shrugged slightly and I asked myself, should they be different?

As I mentioned in chapter 1, our company's core value is transformational connection—connection to music, connection to our agency partners, connection to our clients and their families, and the team's connection to one another. In truth, this is *how* I hope to express all our values to everyone around us—through connection.

To know *what* to blend, you must first identify the outcomes you hope to achieve. The outcomes we choose must be reflected in the feeling that clients, employees, and vendors alike get what our work is all about. If the company's values are not in alignment with the owner's, lack of authenticity and misrepresentation will result in disengagement. Your values must direct the decisions that contribute to the success of your company.

In moments when I've felt tired, I've wondered whether there could be a "perfect blend" for the health entrepreneur that would consistently generate a certain percentage of growth or success. A recipe that could bring forth greater community impact at every turn? A process or template that could be replicated by others? Instinctively, I felt there must be.

To find that perfect blend, I needed to look back to when I started my company and recognize the values I had carried forth through the decades. I reviewed old marketing materials, original business plans, my first budget, archived photos of past clients, and our annual reports. This walk down memory lane showed me that, although I would have done many things differently, our core values were always there.

Although the company's values were at times dimmed due to low confidence and lack of experience, they always found a way to shine through to some degree, even during the start-up years, the economic downturns, and the many moments when I had bouts of self-doubt. There were times when I should have stood up for my values rather than letting them be subsumed by other people's opinions, questions about my youthful competence, and doubts about the viability of my mission. Learning my values junction—my blisspoint—would give me strength. The blend may be unique to each of us, but I believe a successful health entrepreneur needs all three key ingredients—heart, health, and mastery.

Seek Heart

THE HEART OF your work is the heart of your business—your purpose. It makes your business deeply personal, meaningful, and unique; it drives you through the dark and difficult times. It is what your clients ultimately buy in to.

We always seem to rail against the heart when we need to make our next decision. My hunch is that your purpose resonates deeply with your company's core values, and probably goes a step further, aligning with your personal values too.

When we provide a service or product in a manner that makes our customers feel deeply connected to our brand, be it by giving them an opportunity to understand the impact of their purchase or by ensuring every service we provide is focused on their needs, that connection becomes very difficult to break. In a purpose-driven business, we strive to ensure these connections are formed, strengthened, and authenticated. Our business needs to be completely aligned with our purpose, and our purpose needs to fully express this value—our heart.

My company provides a large and growing variety of services in the healthcare and education fields. Each segment uses different terminology and has different needs. For example, one group may focus on music therapy's ability to rehabilitate speech after a stroke, while another looks at how it can boost mood from depression. Our purpose is to bring personalized music therapy to every person we serve, regardless of their age or ability. One way we express our heart is in our service specialization. Personalization can be very expensive; however, because of this model, our customers keep coming back. The service makes them feel good.

As the owner, there are times when I need to reconnect with my purpose. The fastest way for me to connect with our company's heart has been to get back to the front lines. When I step into the field and watch our teamwork, there is no denying the reason for why we do what we do. Taking this time to transport myself into the purpose of my business gives me a tremendous amount of clarity and helps me make decisions. It fuels me with the energy and spirit I need when leading our company into the next stage of its journey.

Solidify Health

HEALTH, IN THE sense that I'm using it here, includes many pieces:

- the health and well-being of the health entrepreneur (review chapter 7 for more details on securing your own health);

- the retention and well-being of our clients;

- the retention and well-being of our staff;

- the well-being of the environment and the community in which we operate;

- our company's resilience and sustainability;

- our current and future financial position.

Jed Emerson introduced the concept of "blended value" as a way to think about the health of a company.[1] Whether for-profit or non-profit, Emerson reminds us to pay attention to the company's economic returns coupled with social and environmental impact over the company's total lifespan. His model suggests that to determine your company's health, you must consider much more than just the bottom line. He suggests that the health of your company includes three important attributes (economic, social, and environmental), and by blending them together the true health of your good work can be evaluated. Let's review these three qualities and how they pertain to the health entrepreneur.

We'll start with *profit*—one of your economic engines. Although it is rarely the primary focus of the health entrepreneur, without profit no real growth can be achieved. Therefore, profit must be one of our health measures. Profit is a significant resource that increases our social impact. As you make profit—whether 1 percent, 5 percent, or 10 percent—you can begin to re-invest this money to benefit your company and, ultimately, your community. In our case, we often re-invest by adding a human resource, a piece of equipment that we can use to better our customer service, an update to our website to ease client use, a new video to bring a story to life, or a new program that we want to test (incurring risk). Wherever this investment is made, we ensure it is planned and executed with the intention to make more profit that we can in turn re-invest into building our next step.

The second attribute is *social capital*. For decades, conventional wisdom and legal definitions clearly separated "doing well" from "doing good." Corporations were for-profit entities that sought to maximize economic value, while public interest groups were non-profits that sought to maximize social or environmental value. But times are changing. More and more organizations invest and find value in corporate social responsibility (CSR), along with other social impact models. Even those with traditional for-profit business models can strive toward a blend of social, environmental, and economic value—or "people, planet, and profit," as many like to think of it. Organizations like ours operate in the middle ground between commercial and social enterprise and create social *and* commercial value. As health entrepreneurs, we fully embrace those seeking our services for health improvements as a big part of our blend. The people we serve, their welfare, and their health are the most important measures we have for the health of our company.

Using Emerson's blended value system, the final attribute required to fully understand the company's health is the *environmental impact*. As health entrepreneurs, this may be something you have not considered often, as most of your efforts have been focused on the people and community you serve. It may take some time to observe your environmental impact and how you can improve upon it. The environmental impact of the healthcare industry is quite significant and as health entrepreneurs we have a role in that. The Institute of Medicine 2013 workshop summary "Public Health Linkages with Sustainability" suggests, "The health sector should lead by example and reduce its ecological footprint to improve global health and the health of the planet."[2] In addition to energy used on-site in the form of heating fuels and electricity, the health-care system uses vast quantities of energy-intensive goods and services, such as pharmaceuticals and medical devices, which require significant energy inputs for their manufacturing. Our instruments, recording devices, and sound sources all fall into this category. Think about the impact that the tools of your trade have on the environment. Vote with your dollars as you decide whether to repair or replace tools and what to do with them when they are no longer suited to your needs or practice.

Making people healthier should be a holistic effort. It doesn't make sense to contribute to some of the major threats to the public's health, to then have to treat them for the consequences down the line.[3] Greenhouse gases are being shown to have negative impacts on human health and livelihoods,[4] and it's important to consider healthcare's several other categories of emissions with negative environmental and public health consequences.

The health entrepreneur who pursues their blisspoint looks at their company's entire health—the potential harm of their choices along with the positive contributions they make. Every healthcare leader first needs to be aware of the company's holistic health, and then consider what measures will mitigate any problems.

Showcase Mastery

EVEN THOUGH IT is perfectly human to be very structured in one area of our lives and quite lax in another, this is not how clients see it—in their minds, we constantly represent our brand, with every interaction, every communication, and every service we offer. This comes back to an idea introduced in chapter 1, about the culture code completing the statement "In everything we do, we believe in..."

Think of it from the client's perspective. Whether purchasing a coffee, finding a new massage therapist, joining a gym, or trying out a new dating website, as customers we have expectations that are either unmet, met, or exceeded during our first encounter with a provider. What brings us back to the same café or gym is being able to count on having an equally good experience every time.

That is why mastery is an important attribute for companies hoping to engage long-term customers. If you become excellent at what you provide and consistent with your level of service, the customer's experience can be replicated time and again. Thus our customers, staff, and community recognize our value, and trust that we will do all we can to ensure they get what they need from us on their first, fifty-seventh, and nine-hundredth visit.

Mastery is not to be confused with professionalism, which mainly focuses on things like dressing suitably for work, showing up on time, doing a good job, being dependable, being ethical, and having advanced degrees and certifications.

Although professionalism is important, mastery goes deeper; it is a blend of experience and expertise, of caring and catering for the needs of those we serve, of attention to detail and awareness of the bigger picture. Achieving mastery requires dedication and consistency. We discussed elements of this mastery in great detail in chapter 2.

Other elements of mastery in running a health service business are:

- a spirit of service;

- a heartfelt purpose;

- a general interest, curiosity, and care for your customers and the global community;

- a commitment to consistently exceeding expectations.

Mastery means going beyond working as professionals. Mastery means being worthy of trust, putting clients first, and maintaining the highest ethical standards when working with others. Interestingly, the outward evidence of these traits may look a lot like dressing suitably for work, showing up on time, and doing a good job—the difference is that true mastery runs much deeper.

As trailblazing health entrepreneurs, it is critical that we don't rest on the laurels of our training and profession, but that our services and products exceed the expectations of every customer, every time we serve them. We need to leave them with the same feeling they loved about us the first time. It's frustrating to spend good money on a service or product that doesn't keep the brand promise. It's even more frustrating to find a great service only to realize the second, third, and fourth time that the great service was just a one-off.

Unfortunately, we are not capable of measuring our own mastery. Modern research on implicit bias tells us that we lack the objectivity to do so. What we can do is consistently pursue proficiency, which requires constant feedback and lifelong learning. The mastery will be felt through your actions and behaviour. You handle problems with the same intensity with which you handle development. The kindness and attention you exhibit to your customers is the same that you give to your team.

The Health Entrepreneur's Rx: Find Your Blisspoint

WE HAVE LEARNED that our blisspoint can be found in the harmony between heart, health, and mastery for you and your business. It is the place where, as a health entrepreneur, you feel the flow in your business, where purpose, sustainability, and momentum reside. When one of the values is missing, you will lose flow and feel stuck.

> When there is heart and health and no mastery =
> only good intentions
> When there is heart and mastery and no health =
> lack of sustainability
> When there is mastery and health and no heart =
> low fulfillment

Think through your personal and professional blisspoint diagram. Are you feeling connected to each of your values? Do you have a sense of the gaps that require some effort to fill? Perhaps you are beginning to feel that the blisspoint concept may also fit in other areas of your life.

When it comes to my personal blisspoint, I have found that the three key values mentioned above continue to apply—with a slight adaptation. My heart holds my deepest reasons for pursuing my passions and purpose; my health is my personal wellness and level of overall mental, physical, and emotional fitness; and my mastery expresses itself in the pursuit of lifelong learning.

The concept of blisspoint gives me a fresh perspective for how to run my business and how to live my life.

Impact Story: How Women Work

How Finding Your Blisspoint Can Lead to Greater Sustainability and Satisfaction

HOW WOMEN WORK (HWW), a social enterprise based in Qatar, was founded to empower women to grow and succeed, to reach hearts and minds, and to break down barriers between cultures and genders.

Like many social enterprises, HWW grew out of a need. Founder Carolin Zeitler felt very alone as a professional woman with ambition and aspirations when she first arrived in Qatar in 2007. So she decided to do something about it.

One by one she befriended other women with ambitions and aspirations. "They were like hidden gems, so inspiring to be around," she said. At some point Carolin thought, wouldn't it be fabulous to have them all in one room together? Imagine the great things that could happen! So as she followed her *heart,* she started These Ladies Mean Business (TLMB), a group that met once a month to give each other feedback on business ideas, presentations, and so on. It was a diverse group, with women of different nationalities, professions, and age groups. Even though their ambitions were different, they all related to one another, because they each wanted to "achieve, build something, and make the world a better place in some small— or big—way."[5]

Seeing how much they benefited from their meetings, the TLMB members decided to make this experience available to more women in Qatar, and How Women Work was born.

Carolin was always looking for the right mix to lead the initiative. She tried many ways—volunteers only, partners, stakeholders—who would get a share of the profit, until she finally found the *health*, the structure, that worked best for the community and for her: a coordinator (basically a project manager), who got a profit share for managing a volunteer team.

Their first initiative was an annual interactive conference that gathered women to exchange experience and knowledge, to network, learn, and know "I am not alone." The conference drew more than 100 women, so it was obvious that there was a need. It soon turned out that meeting once a year was not enough, so demonstrating their *mastery*, HWW started offering more events throughout the year, workshops, mastermind groups, smaller conferences, and retreats.

Carolin worked hard to find the blisspoint—the right mix of live events and online forums, the right mix of professional and personal development content, the right mix of support, coaching, mentoring, and providing opportunities for the women to speak.

The economic situation in Qatar meant that there were many women who didn't need to earn money—their husbands made excellent salaries—but who were craving to work part-time to contribute to something meaningful. How Women Work provided this opportunity, empowering them to grow and succeed, even trusting them with their own projects, giving them ownership of one small aspect. It gave everyone a lot of opportunity for learning, including Carolin, and the coordinator and volunteers.

At the height of HWW under Carolin's leadership, more than three hundred women attended the annual conference with sixty-plus speakers providing talks, workshops, and panel discussions over two days. HWW organized about thirty events during the height of their business.

When, in 2016, Carolin felt the need to leave Qatar for personal reasons, she decided to franchise out HWW Qatar but to retain the rights over the How Women Work brand, maybe to start other branches elsewhere in the world. This time, her ideal mix of trust, intuition, communication, and research, which had served her so well over the years, let her down. Unfortunately, the franchisee transformed the brand to a point where it became unrecognizable to those who used to be part of the community. The core values were compromised, the purpose all but abandoned.

It was difficult for Carolin to witness the brand and its reach dissipate. She realized she had made an error in judgement when she had sought collaboration. However, in true entrepreneurial spirit, Carolin rallied to see an opportunity in the adversity. She could build a fresh brand and create a new mix to focus on supporting social enterprise, contributing to the creation of more sustainable, purpose-driven businesses.

Women's empowerment continues to be a part of it but no longer the sole focus.

For any entrepreneur, finding your blisspoint will help with greater ease in making decisions. Although heart, health, and mastery are the key values for many health entrepreneurs, this blend may not be true for everyone. Take time to pursue and reveal your values, and enjoy the journey.

Questions to Take You to the Next Step

1. What are your three core values?

2. When you meditate on these three values and put them in a Venn diagram, can you see your blisspoint shining through?

3. How does knowing your blisspoint help you and your business?

– 9 –

LEAVE A
LEGACY AHEAD

"The two most important days of your life are
the day you are born and the day you find out why."

MARK TWAIN

T IS HARD to let go and to talk about a world without us in it, isn't it? It's difficult to leave a business you have put your heart and talents into and then leave it behind. Perhaps it's time to look at legacy through a new lens. May I suggest that when you do leave, it's not what you leave behind, it is what you will be leaving *ahead*.

This chapter is about what you can do today that will continue to affect people in the future. It is about moving forward and leaving a legacy ahead—giving the best of yourself until the very end. It's about never letting the challenges or the difficult decisions diminish your good work nor the impact it will have on others.

Like you, I can get tired and overwhelmed by the many decisions, steps, and changes we have had to make in order to fulfill our mission. Not only has my business scaled slowly over many years, but over the same time so has society and its demands, prompting the familiar feeling of "being trapped" by my own creation. There is always more to do; it will never be finished.

Now that we know each other so well, I feel it is time to share another layer of how I have felt since starting my business almost thirty years ago. Although I wouldn't change professions (except maybe to become a Broadway star—I have always had a secret desire to be Elphaba, the green witch in *Wicked*) I have wanted to quit at times; probably close to three or four times a year when things were tough. I always find inspiration in the mission and the people we serve, but all the responsibilities that come with owning a business, ensuring clients and staff get what they need when they need it, can have a very substantial weight.

I was fortunate when the opportunity to address the feeling of being trapped in responsibility presented itself during my last year of business school. During one class, I was asked what happens to my business "post-Jennifer"? Huh? You mean what happens when I can no longer perform my duties as a therapist, manager, and owner? When I no longer have a business identity? What happens to my clients? My team? Our impact? The thought was confusing, exciting, sad, and terrifying in equal parts.

I had a few ideas but I had not taken the time to truly articulate those final next steps.

My professor suggested that I investigate my feelings and write a thoughtful succession plan, as if I were leaving my company within two years.

After much thought, I was surprised I was able to come up with three credible and possible ways I felt I could move my business forward without me. Although each idea would take significant planning and require many steps to execute, the exercise convinced me that I was not trapped, and never was—I just needed to shift my gaze and see the options that were available to me. I have a way out—when I am ready to go.

Prepare for Succession

PERHAPS THE MOST common reason a founder leaves is that, for whatever reason, they feel they can no longer put in the effort required to achieve their desired results.

If we are going to stay true to the message of this book, and to the life of the health entrepreneur, we must talk about some of our deepest fears around business ownership. Much like we do not want to discuss death, we are reluctant to detail what will happen when it is time for us to move on. Sometimes (let's face it, most times) our business becomes very much part of our core identity, it becomes a platform, the stage from which we express so much more than we could have done alone.

So to move from a feeling of ownership to post-owner-ship, we must first ask ourselves, why? Why is this transition important? And, how? How can I achieve this legacy plan with an adaptable, one-win-everything mindset?

During this major transition, success is going to happen, stress is going to present itself, bottlenecks are going to require time to fix, and we need to do what we can to prepare for it all. As health entrepreneurs, we must rise above the stuff we feel and keep progressing. An anonymous quote that plays through my head frequently is "you don't have to have it all figured out to move forward."

A big challenge that start-ups and small businesses face is that a large part of the expertise is stored in the founder's head and nowhere else. Succession planning is ensuring everyone has what they need, when they need it, before you are no longer there to provide the information. So even if you are not planning to leave your business any time soon, you may organize everything enough so that the right person could take over from you—either gradually or suddenly.

To date, you have been wielding the conductor's baton, deciding whether to act or delegate. You have been worrying about the finances, getting the right number of customers to ensure strong revenue, making a good impression, retaining your team, recruiting new talent and serving your clients with care. So when you, the leader, contemplate leaving, you don't feel that you can without hurting something you have birthed, loved, moulded, and poured your heart into.

Things are going to evolve, regardless of whether you remain involved or pass the torch. Change is inevitable. For now, while you are still actively engaged as the leader, ensure the past is valued and the future is secured.

The exercise of planning for that succession day may surprise you. As I began to think about what my succession plan entails, I felt a bit queasy and overwhelmed, even while I was becoming aware that its implementation was still some time away. When you have poured your sweat, tears, money, time, and love into building a successful business for more than twenty-five years, another twenty or so may seem like too much or not enough. Yet there comes a time when we all must think about the future, plan for our replacement, and ultimately move aside for the good of the work.

When my professor suggested that I write a paper detailing our options, here is what I identified:

- Release client portfolios to the current therapists serving them, helping them convert into sole proprietors. Therapists would be trained to manage their own portfolios/ businesses, ensuring job security and continuation of services.

- Sell or merge my business with a larger organization, ensuring that the services would still be available to the public.

- Convert my business into a non-profit. Although the model would significantly shift jobs, clients could still be retained and a level of longevity would be experienced.

If you were presented with the same paper to write, what would you feel is best for your private practice, small business, clients, staff? What options would you be able to implement with hard work, planning, support, and time?

Researchers have found that the smoothest succession plans were those in which the founders (even those who were forced out) remained professional, tried to preserve personal ties with the team, and negotiated exit terms with an eye on the company's well-being.[1] Another interesting conclusion transpired: teams that survived the exit relatively unscathed appeared to gain new learning and they adjusted processes and frameworks to mitigate the future, including major transitions. They seemed to come out stronger for it.

Plan for Transition

AT SOME POINT, you will need to transition out of the business. For me and many founders out there, the exit is not easy to contemplate, but the day will come when it is time to move on to the next great thing, retire, or simply leave because as the visionary leader you know it is the best decision for the company.

We will all face the unique transition considerations of our particular circumstances. For example, when you became a business owner, instead of having one boss you acquired many bosses (your clients) and you were accountable to all of them. Throughout any transition, you are accountable to your brand, your corporate culture, the identity of your business—in short: you, alone, are responsible to preserve your purpose and big dream.

To transition your good work successfully, there are two important steps: prepare and communicate.

To *prepare*, the health entrepreneur must document the desired transition and all the steps that will be required to ensure its success. Whether as a parent, a business owner, or even a volunteer, when it comes to handing over, we tend to have thoughts like "I don't trust anyone else to do this" and "it was my vision from the beginning and I still see where we need to go" and, sadly, "I don't want to be let out to pasture." It is a phenomenon known as "founder's syndrome."

Given the importance of the founder's vision to the vitality of the organization, the thought of the founder leaving seems to shake the very foundations of the business. Even when a company has done all it can to strengthen its teams and systems, sometimes that is still not enough. Large companies also struggle in this area, unable to fully retain their identity and the confidence of their customers when the founder transitions out of the business.

It is, therefore, vital that the transition is documented. You don't have to take large steps, just start with small ones that may entail a contingency succession plan outlining who will lead the company if the leader is suddenly unable (the emergency "hit-by-the-bus" or, more optimistically, the "won-the-lottery" scenario). Then move to more comprehensive succession planning, including ideas around the process of ongoing planning and training for future leadership. Sheri MacMillan of MacMillan Estate Planning suggested that I write a letter of wishes to discuss the key messages and directions I want to pass on to my leadership team if anything should happen to me. This is an exercise I had never considered, and I found it worthwhile for succession/transition planning in general.

When it comes to *communication,* keep in mind your desired outcomes—that you and your team feel prepared, and that you and your clients are not worried. There will always be emotions and stresses whenever change occurs. The health entrepreneur's role is to mitigate the negative emotions and stressors as much as possible. Communicate with everyone affected, laying out the steps they can expect. In a significant transition, the Band-Aid approach (just ripping it off) is not best. Laying out what they can expect (the three to four next steps), your confidence in the process (you know it will work), and the desired outcome (that everyone will be okay) is your most vital role to date. Health entrepreneurs are not just concerned for their clients when they are working directly with them; health entrepreneurs are also concerned for the future care of their clients.

Leave Good Ahead

AT THE END of the day it's not so much about what we leave behind, but what we leave ahead to those who will continue to care for what we have cared about so much. I hope that my team carries forward our awesome mission, systems, and culture, which can be summed up as ideas from the past, hope for the future, and optimism through anything that shows up.

All founders understand that the original business plan is really a living document that will be changed, tested, investigated, and strengthened over time. If we learn from feedback and experience, our original idea will eventually find its most beneficial expression.

Sometimes, when we feel stuck for new ideas, a review of the past can help. Jackie Kennedy understood this when she updated the White House furnishings—not to spend money or to make the house more beautiful, as was the popular opinion in the media, but to reveal ideas of the past, exposing history through artefacts that had been hidden away (at that point there were very few artefacts around the White House that reflected the efforts of people earlier than the 1940s). Since her husband was interested in and strongly affected by history, Jackie felt this would be a great inspiration to him and everyone who visited. As she asserted, "It would be sacrilege merely to redecorate it. It must be restored."[2]

As business owners, we may want to restore our business, to ensure that we are still connected to the original purpose, learning from our past experiences, and building on what has been working well so far. It is not about moving backward but instead reviewing our original intention and aligning that with our current reality, creating an authentic and clear path. Going back to the beginning, to my business plan and the big dream from chapter 1, has kept me on track. A business plan provides not only direction but also inspiration.

Hope is the belief that things could be better and that you can make them so. This message is an important one to impart to your leadership team. Dr. Shane J. Lopez, author of *Making Hope Happen: Create the Future You Want for Yourself and Others*, says that hope is a critical belief for a company's prosperity.[3] Lopez asserts that hope in the workplace accounts for 14 percent of total productivity. Therefore, a company's goals and accompanying strategies must be meaningful and convey the hopeful nature of the mission. According to Lopez, "When we're excited about 'what's next,' we invest more in our daily life, and we can see beyond current challenges."

Did you know that optimistic people work harder? In fact, research has proven that pessimism severely hinders a person's ability to improve their life and work.[4] When we bestow optimism and point out moments that are more beneficial than stressful, our business will become more successful in fulfilling its mission and increasing its profits. Leaving ahead an optimistic mindset can encourage happiness and convey vibrancy, both real and perceived, for many years to come.

The Health Entrepreneur's Rx: Launching a Legacy Ahead

IT HAS COME time to look beyond yourself and plan your final steps.

It is never too early to discuss succession planning. When you are no longer part of the day-to-day operations of this planet—or at least of your business—what that will benefit others will you have left? What foundations have you provided for others to build on?

Whatever the age of the leader or stage of the organization, succession planning is much easier when the founder is involved. So even if you are just starting your business and embarking on your vision as a big-picture thinker, it's important to envision this part of the plan too.

Here are some of the most important items to consider:

- The location of all necessary papers. It is amazing how many items may be available but no one knows where they live.

- Business papers (incorporation papers, insurance information). Please note, when a sole proprietor dies or moves on, the business also closes; however, that does not mean that clients have been looked after. A plan needs to be in place for them.

- Financial statements and access to accounts.

- Access to all accounts (social media too), including usernames and passwords.

- Insurances and lease information.

- Updated procedures and policies, the business and strategic plans, and an understanding of the owner's wishes for the company.

- Client files and the key or password required to access them.

- A list of vendors for ease of purchasing or procuring supplies.

- A list of key stakeholders and contacts.

An exit plan engages the founder in a deep exercise that stretches beyond business knowledge, tenacity, and strength. It isn't just logistics such as updating your business plan and policies, clarifying key performance measures, tightening up financials, and refining and strengthening the SWOT analysis. A departure strategy invites emotional growth. When I developed my final steps, I needed to address the recurring feelings of being trapped and obligated by my own creation. I needed to create a plan to open the door to the greatest transition my company would see since its inception.

Surprisingly, at the end of this process, I formed a detailed plan, and with it I had feelings of relief closely joined by a resurgence of energy for more good work. I still had more in me to do, but now I had a greater sense of what needed to be done and an improved perspective of how to do it.

In many ways my company has achieved the mission I set out with so many years ago. We created a sustainable for-profit-for-purpose business that has meant the world to me and hopefully to the thousands we have served and continue to.

However, this exercise has convinced me that I am not done. It is time to look deep within myself and find what is next.

It is not just the future I need to look to; it is the past, ideas that haven't yet come to fruition; it is the present, the current needs of our clients, the gaps in our society that continue to exist. I trust opportunities will continue to present themselves, along with the necessary next steps—and the joy of pursuing them.

Impact Story:
Pavarotti Music Centre in Mostar

How to Bring Your Dream to
Life for Many Generations to Come

TWENTY YEARS AGO, the Pavarotti Music Centre was established in an old building of an elementary school in Mostar, Bosnia and Herzegovina. It was an initiative of the charity War Child, U.K., and generously supported by Luciano Pavarotti, along with many more celebrities. The vision was to establish a music centre that would support the healing of a traumatized people, especially children, after a war that almost eradicated an entire ethnic group. The music centre was created to help heal the enormous amount of pain and regret left behind in the aftermath.

The music centre found its students playing in the rubble of bombed-out homes, living in basements to escape the shelling, alongside the bodies of their parents, who had been killed by the bombing. The music centre was meant to give them a safe space to make noise, rediscover joy, and—for the most traumatized—begin to articulate their feelings, with the support of music therapists trained to help in that way.

A journalist revisiting the site twenty years later was reconnected with some of the children she had interviewed during their darkest days. Amir, who had become an artist, and Jasmina, who was joyfully getting married, both remembered the centre as a place that gave children an opportunity to play and disagree about normal things like tastes in music rather than having to think constantly about war and its gruesome consequences.

Although Mostar itself continues to be deeply divided, the music centre continues with its legacy to make a difference: to be a pillar of healing and a bridge for people of different backgrounds.

Our legacy, what we leave ahead, is something we often will not fully realize. The true legacy may happen long after we have gone. In some ways, you must trust that the work you have put into your succession plan, and the feelings you have infused in your company, will somehow linger far into the many transitions and growth moments of your business's future.

Questions to Take You to the Final Step

1. When you consider leaving your company, how do you feel?

2. What are the most significant steps you must accomplish in order to transition successfully, with as little disruption to your business as possible?

3. What three feelings do you wish to leave ahead?

END ON A HIGH NOTE

"Never look down to test the ground before
taking your next step; only he who keeps his eye fixed
on the far horizon will find the right road."

DAG HAMMARSKJÖLD

N THE EARLY 1900s, five courageous women, Henrietta Muir Edwards, Nellie McClung, Louise McKinney, Emily Murphy, and Irene Parlby, faced violence and adversity when they were trying to affirm that women were "persons" under the law. Their bravery, purposeful fight, and ultimate win gave many women all across Canada a voice, and the opportunity and access they needed to make a difference. More women came after them and continued the fight until 1960 when all woman in Canada had the same rights and freedoms.[1]

To this day, the Famous 5 Foundation has continued the pursuit for equality by bridging the leadership gap for women to ensure that no future generation experiences inequality, double standards, or stereotypes of gender. Today their mission continues to inspire confidence and leadership through insight, resources, and the skills training necessary to correct the historic inequalities.

Though the pursuit of equality for women (equal pay and opportunity) has not yet been fully realized, there have been many steps to get this far. Each has furthered the goal, and each is necessary but not necessarily sufficient.

Like the pursuit for equality for women, the pursuit for acceptance of the health entrepreneur, the disintegration of the judgement that says that profit is the only measure of a successful business, is still in progress. And you too could be part of the movement, one of those who takes the necessary step that moves us all to the next level.

As you have learned, I have ebbed and flowed on the spectrum of love I have had for my business. Yet by maintaining focus on developing something beyond myself, whether it be a small private practice that reaches twenty people a week in a meaningful way or developing a service-based company that reaches thousands a month, all of us are contributing to the greater human condition by helping create a different way of doing business.

When I was in the sixth grade, my teacher announced that the world population had reached four-and-a-half billion people. Around the year 2011, it rose to seven billion, and that number will increase to around nine billion in my lifetime. These numbers are staggering, putting a lot of pressure on the planet but also on individuals as we navigate the stress and anxieties that come from having less space and more needs. In short, there are a lot of people to help.

Service-based businesses, regardless of the type, can help support this growing population. We can create employment, boost the economy, and hopefully make a more positive experience for everyone who encounters us and the good work we provide.

So what is your next step? Knowing your next move is not about assessing the profit a project will bring us but instead going deeper within, to your own personal profit, your values, your character, and your skills, to use them in a way you feel good about. Taking care of your business is the best way to take care of others.

I have been one of the fortunate ones: I learned early on who I was fighting for. As time went by, I realized that fighting isn't all I am doing—I am clearing a new path alongside many of you. I have moved through many mistakes and a host of opportunities. I have tried new ideas, some that have worked well and others that I am not sure I ever want to think about let alone try again. I have cried many tears over decisions I felt were too difficult to make, and felt a tremendous amount of lightheartedness and joy when one of those difficult decisions worked. I have not done any of this alone, but with the help of a supportive husband, dear friends and family, a great team, advisors, mentors, client partners, and networking groups. For all these people I am grateful.

You will face moments when you feel stuck, torn, and unsure. You will always be faced with ethical dilemmas, conflicts, disagreements, and difficult transitions. Keep your lens on your clients. Let them help guide your gaze to what direction to take. Trust your expertise, your learnings, your education, your professionalism, and perhaps most importantly your intuition to guide you through the next step. When we move together, we have our best chance of moving ahead.

Additional Tips for Doing Good

A GOOD COMPANY always offers a little bit extra—even when the client thought the relationship was over. Here are a few extra tips that I hope will make your life as a health entrepreneur easier and your company grow effortlessly.

Buy the best chair you can find. You'll probably use your chair more than any other piece of office equipment, including your computer, so don't settle; love your chair, love your office.

Purchase carefully. We vote with our dollars. When you do buy a resource, remember to buy it to last and to support the causes you value. Procuring your resources from businesses that share your values will not only strengthen your business but also theirs.

Nurture relationships. Understand that relationships are more important than contracts. Business deals are relationships between people. The signed piece of paper is important, but it's merely the result of the relationship, not the cause. If the relationship crumbles, the contract won't save you. I have dumped some contracts to preserve relationships. Go with your gut and ask yourself how important that agency or individual is to you. Do you need to stick to your guns or can you be flexible?

Set deadlines when you feel stuck. Take time with your daily, weekly, monthly, and annual calendar. Although dates can be moved, putting in a few key dates to look forward to, and more importantly plan for, can help you find that whisk of motivation when you need it most. Meetings with key stakeholders, annual surveys, public presentations, team meetings, company socials, and significant anniversaries can all be put in the calendar a year in advance and help provide a frame to your year.

Think for yourself. Do your own research, draw your own conclusions, set your own course, and stick to your purpose.

Fail faster. You are going to screw up. You may even screw up a lot. Don't worry so much about failing—it is just a by-product of learning and growth. Learn to fail faster so you can get back on the horse and move forward.

Become so organized that you surprise even yourself. You'll never achieve perfection. However, if you are not well organized, punctual, and dependable, rest assured you're competing with someone who is.

Be consistent. You don't have to do what everyone else is doing. If I were to write another book or another speech, it would be about a key skill that business has taught me—to be consistent. Not just for an hour or a day but over the long haul.

Stay accessible and recognizable. Having numerous websites, varying corporate colours, or different phone numbers is confusing—especially at the beginning. Ensure your business cards are accurate and don't change your brand often. Give people time to get to know you and remember you.

Look after yourself. Adopt the routines that give you your desired outcomes. Do whatever it takes to look after yourself, including having a rich social life or ample alone time, whatever fuels you.

Integrate your life into your work. Be authentic. People know when they are hanging out with someone who is putting on a persona. You should never feel like you are acting, at work or at home.

Know when to raise your rates. Here are some indicators that it's time:
- You've improved your service and/or skills.
- The supply and demand have changed.

- You want to work fewer hours.
- You are testing to gain more information.
- You want to reposition yourself (for example, move from technician to consultant).

Avoid common mistakes. These include:

- not testing;
- not seeking feedback;
- not raising rates at all;
- changing rates too often.

Don't skip the finances. Two of the best business decisions I ever made were hiring a bookkeeper and putting myself on salary.

NOTES

Chapter 1: Drive Your Dream

[1] Jim C. Collins and Jerry I. Porras, "BHAG—Big Hairy Audacious Goal," Jim Collins, accessed November 21, 2018, https://www.jimcollins.com/article_topics/articles/BHAG.html.

[2] Warren Bennis, "The Secrets of Great Groups," *Leader to Leader* 3 (2007): 29–33.

[3] "Millennials Plan to Redefine the C-Suite Says New American Express Survey," American Express, November 29, 2017, https://about.americanexpress.com/press-release/millennials-plan-redefine-c-suite-says-new-american-express-survey.

[4] Danny Coyle, *The Culture Code: The Secrets of Highly Successful Groups* (New York: Bantam Books, 2018).

[5] "Culture," WestJet, accessed November 21, 2018, https://www.westjet.com/en-ca/about-us/jobs/culture.

[6] Teresa Amabile and Steve Kramer, "To Give Your Employees Meaning, Start with Mission," *Harvard Business Review*, December 19, 2012, https://hbr.org/2012/12/to-give-your-employees-meaning.

[7] Mark Arnoldy, "Why I Wrote the For-Impact Culture Code," LinkedIn, July 21, 2014, https://www.linkedin.com/pulse/20140721160549-230361209-why-i-wrote-the-for-impact-culture-code.

[8] Angela Randolph quoted in Barbara Haislip, "An Entrepreneur's Story Can Be the Perfect Marketing Tool," *Wall Street Journal*, April 30, 2017,

https://www.wsj.com/articles/an-entrepreneurs-story-can-be-the-perfect-marketing-tool-1493604360.

9 "About Bombas," Bombas, accessed November 21, 2018, https://bombas.com/pages/about-us.

10 Shelley Levitt, "How Bombas Socks Survived the 'Shark Tank,'" Success, September 9, 2016, https://www.success.com/how-bombas-socks-survived-the-shark-tank.

Chapter 2: Strengthen Your Expertise

1 Malcom Gladwell, *Outliers: The Story of Success* (New York: Little, Brown and Company, 2008), 239.

2 Mark Murphy, "The Dunning-Kruger Effect Shows Why Some People Think They're Great Even When Their Work Is Terrible," *Forbes*, January 24, 2017, https://www.forbes.com/sites/markmurphy/2017/01/24/the-dunning-kruger-effect-shows-why-some-people-think-theyre-great-even-when-their-work-is-terrible.

3 Margaret Rouse, "Lean Startup," TechTarget, April 2018, https://searchcio.techtarget.com/definition/Lean-startup.

4 Amy J.C. Cuddy, Matthew Kohut, and John Neffinger, "Connect, Then Lead," *Harvard Business Review*, July/August 2013, https://hbr.org/2013/07/connect-then-lead.

5 "The Amazing Village in the Netherlands Just for People with Dementia," Twisted Sifter, February 4, 2015, https://twistedsifter.com/2015/02/amazing-village-in-netherlands-just-for-people-with-dementia.

Chapter 3: Maximize Your Message

1 "Recommendations from Friends Remain Most Credible Form of Advertising Among Consumers," Neilson, September 28, 2015, https://www.nielsen.com/eu/en/press-room/2015/recommendations-from-friends-remain-most-credible-form-of-advertising.html.

2 Andy Sernovitz, *Word of Mouth Marketing: How Smart Companies Get People Talking* (Austin: Greenleaf Book Group, 2012).

[3] Jim Burns, "No Marketing Momentum? What Now?" Avitage, accessed November 21, 2018, https://avitage.com/no-marketing-momentum-what-now.

[4] See Lisa Sasevich, www.lisasasevich.com.

[5] Jennifer Buchanan, *Tune In: A Music Therapy Approach to Life* (Austin: Hugo House Publishers, 2015), 1.

[6] Jim Adler quoted in Thomas Hobbs, "Toyota on Its Plan to Bring Robots into the Home," *Marketing Week*, November 20, 2017, https://www.marketingweek.com/2017/11/20/toyota-on-bringing-robots-into-the-home.

[7] Doug Moore (senior manager of Future Mobility Business and Technology for Human Support), in conversation with the author, November 2018.

[8] "Population Ages 65 and Above (% of Total)," World Bank Group, accessed November 21, 2018, https://data.worldbank.org/indicator/sp.pop.65up.to.zs.

Chapter 4: Scale for Impact

[1] Matt Roberge, "Why Is Scaling A Service-Based Business So Difficult?" *Salt Lake City Bookkeeping Blog*, February 20, 2013, https://www.slcbookkeeping.com/blog/bid/113093/Why-Is-Scaling-A-Service-Based-Business-So-Difficult.

[2] Alexander Osterwalder and Yves Pigneur, *Business Model Generation* (Hoboken: John Wiley & Sons, 2010).

[3] "Clan Buchanan History," ScotClans, accessed November 21, 2018, https://www.scotclans.com/scottish-clans/clan-buchanan/buchanan-history.

[4] "From Our Family to Yours," Tom's of Maine, accessed November 21, 2018, https://www.tomsofmaine.com/the-backstory.

[5] See Jim Collins, "Good to Great," Jim Collins, October 2001, https://jimcollins.com/article_topics/articles/good-to-great.html.

[6] Brian Tracy, *Motivation*, The Brian Tracy Success Library (New York: AMACOM, 2013), 12–16.

[7] Jacqueline Peters, *High Performance Relationships: The Heart and Science Behind Success at Work and Home* (Calgary: InnerActive Leadership Associates Inc., 2015).

[8] Michael True quoted in Penny Loretto, "The Value of Offering Paid Internships," The Balancecareers, October 15, 2018, https://www.thebalancecareers.com/the-golden-age-of-internships-1987140.

[9] "For-Profit Social Ventures in Waterloo Region: An Exploratory Study," Capacity Waterloo Region, 2010, https://capacitycanada.ca/wp-content/uploads/2014/08/Capacity-Canada-Social-Ventures-Report.pdf.

[10] Tom Dawkins quoted in Nathan Chan, "51: How to Start Your Own Social Enterprise and Make a Big Impact with StartSomeGood's founder Tom Dawkins," Foundr, July 27, 2015, https://foundr.com/tom-dawkins.

[11] Chantal Fernandez, "How SoulCycle Scales Community," Business of Fashion, December 1, 2007, https://www.businessoffashion.com/articles/voices/how-soulcycle-scales-community.

Chapter 5: Build In the Spirit of Equity

[1] See "Dr. Cynthia Bruce," Acadia University Education, accessed November 21, 2018, https://education.acadiau.ca/faculty-and-staff/dr-cynthia-bruce.html.

[2] Evan Chacker, "An Entrepreneur's Guide to Using the 'One-Win-Everything' Negotiating Technique," Virgin, May 23, 2017, https://www.virgin.com/entrepreneur/entrepreneurs-guide-using-one-win-everything-negotiating-technique.

[3] Lisa Delpit, *"Multiplication Is for White People": Raising Expectations for Other People's Children* (New York: The New Press, 2012), 77.

[4] Zaretta Hammond, *Culturally Responsive Teaching and the Brain: Promoting*

Authentic Engagement and Rigor Among Culturally and Linguistically Diverse Students (Thousand Oaks, CA: Corwin, 2015), 80.

5 "Obama Administration Advances Efforts to Protect Health of U.S. Communities Overburdened by Pollution," The White House: President Barack Obama, August 4, 2011, https://www.doi.gov/news/pressreleases/Obama-Administration-Advances-Efforts-to-Protect-Health-of-UScommunities-Overburdened-by-Pollution.

6 Emanuel Kay, Herbert H. Meyer, and John R. P. French, "Effects of Threat in a Performance Appraisal Interview," *Journal of Applied Psychology* 49, no. 5 (November 1965): 311–17, http://dx.doi.org/10.1037/h0022522.

7 Jennifer Buchanan, "5 Ways to Build the Spirit of Equity into Your Small Business," LinkedIn, July 11, 2017, https://www.linkedin.com/pulse/5-ways-build-spirit-equity-your-small-business-buchanan-mba-mta.

8 Katherine Power quoted in Michelle McQuigge, "Better Workplace Accessibility for Canadians with Disabilities Would Boost Economic Growth: Study," *Globe and Mail*, February 25, 2018, https://www.theglobeandmail.com/news/national/better-workplace-accessibility-for-canadians-with-disabilities-would-boost-economic-growth-study/article38105222.

Chapter 6: Clear the Path

1 *Cambridge Dictionary*, s.v. "mindset," accessed November 21, 2018, https://dictionary.cambridge.org/dictionary/english/mindset.

2 Carol Dweck, *Mindset: How You Can Fulfil Your Potential* (London: Robinson, 2012).

3 "What Is Social Purpose Business," Futurpreneur Canada, accessed November 21, 2018, https://www.futurpreneur.ca/en/resources/social-purpose-business/articles/what-is-social-purpose-business.

4 "Social Enterprise Terminology," The Institute for Social Entrepreneurs, accessed November 21, 2018, http://www.socialent.org/Social_Enterprise_Terminology.htm.

[5] *The Canadian Encyclopedia*, s.v. "Recession of 2008–09 in Canada," by Stephen Gordon, last edited October 24, 2017, https://www.thecanadianencyclopedia.ca/en/article/recession-of-200809-in-canada.

[6] Lauren Moraski, "Ashton Kutcher Gives Life Advice at Teen Choice Awards," CBS News, August 11, 2013, https://www.cbsnews.com/news/ashton-kutcher-gives-life-advice-at-teen-choice-awards.

[7] Zita Cobb quoted in Rosanna Caira, "Zita Cobb Talks Social Entrepreneurship at Fogo Island Inn," Hotelier, June 12, 2015, http://www.hoteliermagazine.com/zita-cobb-talks-social-entrepreneurship-at-fogo-island-inn.

Chapter 7: Secure Your Health

[1] "Constitution of WHO: Principles," World Health Organization, accessed November 21, 2018, https://www.who.int/about/mission/en.

[2] "The Ottawa Charter for Health Promotion," World Health Organization, accessed November 21, 2018, http://www.who.int/healthpromotion/conferences/previous/ottawa/en .

[3] Jordan S. Kassalow, "Why Health Is Important to U.S. Foreign Policy," Council on Foreign Relations, April 19, 2001, https://www.cfr.org/report/why-health-important-us-foreign-policy.

[4] Marc G. Berman, John Jonides, and Stephen Kaplan, "The Cognitive Benefits of Interacting with Nature," *Psychological Science* 19, no. 12 (December 1, 2008): 1207–12, https://doi.org/10.1111/j.1467-9280.2008.02225.x.

[5] "Why Sleep Matters," Harvard Medical School, accessed November 7, 2018, video, 6:13, http://healthysleep.med.harvard.edu/video/sleep07_matters.

[6] Alison G. Walton, "Seven Ways Meditation Can Actually Change the Brain," *Forbes*, February 9, 2015, https://www.forbes.com/sites/alicegwalton/2015/02/09/7-waysmeditation-canactually-changethebrain/#185dceba1465.

[7] Kelly McGonigal quoted in Thai Nguyen, "10 Benefits for Entrepreneurs that Make Time for Silence and Solitude," Entrepreneur, May 26, 2015, https://www.entrepreneur.com/article/246503.

[8] Sam Harris, "A Contemplative Science," Huffington Post, May 25, 2011, https://www.huffingtonpost.com/sam-harris/a-contemplative-science_b_15024.html.

[9] Jonathan Schooler quoted in Thai Nguyen, "10 Important Reasons to Start Making Time for Silence, Rest and Solitude," Huffington Post, November 3, 2014, https://www.huffpost.com/entry/10-important-reasons-to-s_b_6035662.

[10] Carnegie Mellon University, "How Stress Influences Disease: Study Reveals Inflammation as the Culprit," ScienceDaily, April 2, 2012, www.sciencedaily.com/releases/2012/04/120402162546.htm.

[11] Anapum Pant, "The Role of Wind in a Tree's Life," Awesci, accessed November 21, 2018, http://awesci.com/the-role-of-wind-in-a-trees-life.

[12] Walter Mischel, The Marshmallow Test: Mastering Self-Control (London: Corgi, 2015), 126.

[13] Mark Zuckerberg, "Mark Zuckerberg's Commencement Address at Harvard," (speech, Harvard University, Cambridge, MA, May 25, 2017), https://news.harvard.edu/gazette/story/2017/05/mark-zuckerbergs-speech-as-written-for-harvards-class-of-2017/.

[14] Brené Brown, Daring Greatly: How the Courage to Be Vulnerable Transforms the Way We Live, Love, Parent, and Lead (New York: Avery, 2012).

[15] See Mihaly Csikszentmihalyi, Flow: The Psychology of Optimal Experience (New York: Harper & Row, 1990).

[16] Bruce Kumar Frantzis, "The 70 Percent Rule in Tai Chi: An Essential Principle," in The Big Book of Tai Chi (London: Thorsons, 2003), 35–37.

Chapter 8: Find Your Blisspoint

[1] "Jed Emerson," Blended Value, accessed November 7, 2018, http://www.blendedvalue.org/about-jed-emerson/.

[2] Institute of Medicine, "Public Health Linkages with Sustainability: Workshop Summary" (Washington, DC: The National Academies Press, 2013), https://doi.org/10.17226/18375.

[3] Matthew J. Eckelman and Jodi Sherman, "Environmental Impacts of the U.S. Health Care System and Effects on Public Health," PLOS One, June 9, 2016, https://doi.org/10.1371/journal.pone.0157014.

[4] A.J. McMichael, R.E. Woodruff, and S. Hales, "Climate Change and Human Health: Present and Future Risks," The Lancet 367, no. 9513 (March 11, 2006): 859–69, https://doi.org/10.1016/s0140-6736(06)68079-3.

[5] Carolin Zeitler, in conversation with the author, February 2018. See also Carolin Zeitler, How Women Succeed: Inspiring Women to Create Their Own Success (Qatar: How Women Work, 2014).

Chapter 9: Leave a Legacy Ahead

[1] Rieke Dibbern, Rebecca Preller, Nicola Breugst, and Holger Patzelt, "Dynamics of Co-Founder Exits in Entrepreneurial Teams," Academy of Management Proceedings 2017, no. 1, October 30, 2017, https://doi.org/10.5465/ambpp.2017.208.

[2] Jacqueline Kennedy quoted in Hugh Sidey, "Everything Must Have a Reason for Being There," Life, September 1961, 57.

[3] Dr. Shane J. Lopez, Making Hope Happen: Create the Future You Want for Yourself and Others (New York: Simon & Schuster, 2013).

[4] Fiona Parashar, "The Psychology of Optimism and Pessimism: Theories and Research Findings," Positive Psychology, October 24, 2009, http://positivepsychology.org.uk/optimism-pessimism-theory.

Conclusion: End on a High Note

[1] "The 'Persons' Case," Famous Five Foundation, accessed November 21, 2018, http://www.famou5.ca/the-persons-case-1.

ACKNOWLEDGEMENTS

THANK YOU TO Page Two for taking me over the finishing line with wisdom, skill, and enthusiasm. The entire process exceeded my expectations. Special gratitude to Amanda Lewis, my editor and now friend, and Jesse Finkelstein, who is a living example of someone leading a values-driven business.

I would also like to thank Linda Dessau and Carolin Zeitler, who helped me transition from school papers to blogs to the very first draft of the book. It has been the very best experience for writing a book.

Below is a compilation of all the people who have made and continue to make a difference to me personally and professionally. This is also an example of the final activity that I encourage all health entrepreneurs to do.

Recognition is one of the best investments you can make in creating value for you as an individual, and for your organization. It is an expression of the one-win-everything model, as it creates good feelings that resonate far and wide into good work.

My Closest Partner

JAMES: YOU WALK beside me always, through every step of this book, and for more than half my life. You have helped me clear the path. I love you.

Family—People Who Are Always There

MERRICK

BRAEDAN

MOM

ANDREA

AND EVERYONE ELSE I have spent Thanksgiving dinner with, I love you all very much.

Friends—People Who Know Us Best and Love Us Anyway

MICHELLE OUCHAREK-DEO

CHARLENE BEARDEN

FIONA MCCOLL

DEBBIE LAKE

LAUREL YOUNG

MELANIE MCDONALD

ERIN BORCZON

Mentors—People Who We Seek Advice From

THE BUSINESS DEN—JACQUELINE Peters, Bruce Sellery, Jaclyn Fimrite, Dennis and Katie Plintz—you helped get me this far.

Other wise mentors, just to name a very few, who have advised me along the way and helped me with the perspective

I needed to keep on keeping on are Fran Herman, Ken Wilson, and Don Bialik.

Mavens—People Who Are Experts and Inform Our Work

MY SOCIAL MEDIA informants. All those whose incredible accomplishments and articles inspire me along the way, yet we have never met, including but not limited to the entrepreneurs, health entrepreneurs, socialpreneurs, and researchers I follow from @musictherapy and @jenniferbuchananinc. You keep me informed daily and are friends when I feel alone in the work.

I would also like to thank all the educators who asked me the right questions at the right time, making me think, all the while challenging me, supporting me, to take the next step whether I felt completely ready or not.

Champions—People Who Believe in Us and Tell Others About Us

KRISTA HERMANSON

MEGAN STANLEY

JUDY STAWYNYCHKO

PATRICIA MORGAN

JANET FEDOR

SHARON MOFFATT

You have helped me significantly grow as a speaker, author, business owner, and therapist. It has been your faith in me that has helped me believe in myself when I have felt tired and uncertain.

Staff and Clients—People We Serve
and Who Reward Us In Return

SHANNON ROBINSON (WHO could have been under every one of the above headers) and the entire team at JB Music Therapy Inc. It is an honour to work alongside you.

My coaching clients. What a gift you are to work with. Thank you for making such a huge difference in the world and allowing me to be a small piece of that journey.

And far from last, definitely not least... each and every one of the music therapy clients, agencies, and organizations that I have had the privilege to work with, for without you, this book would not have been written.

ABOUT THE AUTHOR

JENNIFER BUCHANAN is a health entrepreneur in the truest sense of the word. Since becoming a certified music therapist almost three decades ago, she has witnessed the music therapy industry shift from not being considered an industry at all to becoming a legislated profession. As a leading expert, Buchanan has served hundreds of organizations with her team at JB Music Therapy, which she founded in 1991. JB Music Therapy has thrice been nominated for the Community Impact Award by the Calgary Chamber of Commerce. Buchanan was also the former president of the Canadian Association of Music Therapists (1998 to 2001, 2013 to 2015) She is recognized as an esteemed leader in bridging academic research in music medicine and the public, and has spoken on many media outlets as well as internationally to numerous educational, healthcare, and government organizations. She is currently on the board of directors with the Famous 5 Foundation and looks forward to visiting more places and meeting more interesting people on her life's journey.

VISIT WWW.JENNIFERBUCHANAN.CA FOR keynotes, seminars, personalized online coaching, and classes to support your *Wellness Incorporated* dream journey and the necessary self-care required along the way.

THANK YOU FOR taking the time to read this book. I look forward to continuing the conversation about your good work.

Jennifer

CPSIA information can be obtained
at www.ICGtesting.com
Printed in the USA
LVHW032030210119
604681LV00005B/459/P

9 780973 944631